Welcome To The Real World

Godfrey Rust

Collected poems & performance pieces
1980-2000

WORDSOUT

First published in Great Britain November 2000.

ISBN 0-9520212-1-8

The scripture quotations on page 115 and 163 are taken from the
HOLY BIBLE, NEW INTERNATIONAL VERSION. Copyright
© 1973, 1978, 1984 by International Bible Society.

Cover design by Julianna Franchetti and Chris Gander.

Production by Chris Gander Design Associates, St Andrews
House, 17 St Andrews Road, Croydon CR0 1AB.

Printed and bound in Great Britain by Cox & Wyman, Reading.

Published by Wordsout Publications, 14 Gloucester Road,
London W5 4JB, United Kingdom. Telephone 020 8579 8655.
email admin@wordsout.co.uk Website:www.wordsout.co.uk

UK trade distribution by Perivale Christian Distributors,
184 Horsenden Lane South, Perivale, Middx UB6 7NT.
Telephone sales (trade orders) 020 8998 2940.
Telephone sales (credit card) 020 8998 2989.
Internet sales (credit card) www.wordsout.co.uk.
Mail order from Wordsout Publications (address above).

All proceeds from the sale of this book go to the Nineveh Trust to
support Christian work in developing and deprived areas.

Contents

Welcome to the real world (2000)

Introduction

A poem is a door between different worlds.

A good poem opens from the everyday world in which it is being read or listened to, onto a world of imagination in which surprising things happen and in which improbable things exist side by side.

If you are lucky, as you stand in the doorway that the poem has opened you will find that this glimpse of another world changes—sometimes forever—your understanding of the everyday world with which you thought you were familiar.

Which of these worlds is the most real?

This book contains pieces written over a period of twenty years. My first, home-produced, collection *The Place Where Socks Go* appeared in 1985 in response to demand for copies of poems performed at concerts with Geoff Shattock. This grew up into *Breaking the Chains* (Word, 1992) which included *The sailing of the ark*, and is reprinted here unchanged apart from minor corrections and some updated references. The remaining poems, written since 1992, are published here under the title *Welcome to the real world* for the first time.

Poems are doors that have locks. You will bring to them the keys of your experience, and because your history and mine are not the same, not all these doors will open, or open completely, for you. Anyone over forty and living in the UK will find that *Come on in, the sofa's lovely* opens (all too easily!) at the first nudge.

But unless, for example, you happen to know (and care) that Galileo, using the first telescope, discovered that Jupiter had its own orbiting moons at a time when more than a thousand years of dogmatic belief—and the Inquisition—had insisted that the earth was the centre of the universe, then the lock on the poem on page 238 will fail to turn for you.

This is not a book of religious or devotional verse, but its perspective is clearly Christian. There will be those who look in it for an underlying theology, to place it, for example, in an evangelical, or liberal, or mystical tradition. There is a binding logic to be found here: that the life, death and resurrection of Jesus were both historical and spiritual events, and are the defining expressions of God's relationship with humanity.

But a very big change is going on around us. At the beginning of the 21st century we find ourselves firmly rooted in postmodernism, the first radically new phase of western culture for over half a millennium (though to be firmly rooted in anything postmodern is, of course, something of a contradiction in terms).

Propositions have given way to stories, positions to views. We have become defined by what we consume, not what we produce. Opinion has supplanted truth, in our debating as much as our advertising. The exercise of choice has become our principal form of worship, and we are tolerant of anything except dogma. Our identities dissolve into a series of disconnected images—we are what we seem.

This is a dramatic shift in our culture. The ground was prepared by scientists: Einstein (with Relativity) and Heisenberg (with quantum mechanics) discovered early in the 20th century that the workings of our universe are weird—and its scale huge—beyond all imagination. Both time and space are relative and unpredictable. More disturbing than that, at the extreme limits of speed and mass, time and space become impossible to tell apart. In the everyday world, nothing is really the way it seems.

The comforting certainty of Newton's physics is gone for ever, and with the gates of modernism fatally breached it took only the combination of economic prosperity and mass communication to sack the city entirely and set up consumerism in the Holy of Holies:

>   —this abomination
> that brings desolation, this god of matter
>
> to whose altar we have been dragged
> smiling to be sacrificed.

(The sailing of the ark, sonnet 11)

Now, driven by global commercial competition and the 24-hour casino of the stock market, we are rushing headlong into the next phase, that of the Internet, in which the "real" is replaced by the virtual. The pace of technological development in computing and medicine over the next century will be staggering: its consequences are unimaginable. Everything, including life itself, is up for grabs.

All of this deals body blows to the "real world" of our conventional thought and behaviour. Formal Christianity is in the firing line as much, if not more, than anything else. 21st century postmodernism smiles blankly and ironically at evangelical phariseeism and declines to be interested in its tedious drawing of borderlines.

Of course this is threatening. God as an objective person is deeply unfashionable: in postmodern thought, everything is a *view*. Already dismissed by philosophy as irrational and science as unknowable, God is now redefined by popular culture as a consumer option.

But postmodernism is also liberating for Christianity. It is no coincidence that "Jesus chose the parable", and the postmodern emphasis on stories rather than creeds brings us closer to the 1st century than, say, the mid 20th.

One of the most empowering features of postmodernism is that it is no respecter of person or tradition. It is not afraid to say when the emperor has no clothes, or is at least clad in extremely threadbare underwear. Christians have been doing the same and, having found they have not been struck down with a thunderbolt for voicing their doubts and concerns, have been encouraged to believe that there may be other ways to embrace radical discipleship other than those formulated in the middle of the twentieth century around western prosperity and the Four Spiritual Laws.

The sailing of the ark documents my own journey into postmodern Christianity. As I wrote in the original introduction to this poem, I had found modern evangelicalism a creed spelled out in black and white, and the God of the manger and the wilderness was not to be pinned down so easily.

Postmodernism does not say there *is* no objective truth: it only says that, if there is, we can never know it. Postmodern Christianity agrees that we can only know truth "as in a mirror, darkly"; but it has faith, hope and love as means of access to the real world. Parable and metaphor—that is, poetry—provide some glimpses of it.

In this book, ideas in different poems sometimes appear at odds with one another; but life is not tidy, and for precedents I point to Job, the Psalms and Ecclesiastes; more recently to Gerard Manley Hopkins' "terrible sonnets" and to James K Baxter, whose fractured sonnet form I borrowed for the *ark*.

The style of these pieces varies according to their origin and purpose. Many were written with performance in mind (after more than a decade of commissions for Christmas Carol services I think I have covered the Nativity from every possible angle with the exception of the donkey). For those who wish to read or perform some of these pieces in worship services or other events I have provided some notes and an index of themes at the end of the book.

Throughout 1999 I was determined not to write a Millennium poem. *Song at the start of a century* is it.

For ideas, encouragement, criticism and (unpaid!) commissions I am grateful to Mark Bratton, Isobel Montgomery Campbell, Stan and Judith Dakin, Gill Dallow, Colin and Mary Duckworth, James and Mary Lazarus, Donald McRobbie, John and Carina Persson, Jackie Runcorn, Geoff Shattock, Joanna Whitfield and especially to my wife Tessa, children Emma, Joel and Adam, and mother Joan.

For help and advice in the production and marketing of this book I am also indebted to Julianna Franchetti, Chris Gander, Colin and Steve Taylor and Julie Woods.

All three sections of this book come to their conclusive points at the cross. Christ's instruction that "he who would find his life must lose it" goes beyond both reason and common sense: love is, quite literally, absurd.

But I find some things inescapable: that God's behaviour is subversive; that all important truth is paradoxical; and that love in the form of self-sacrificial forgiveness is the most powerful force in the universe. These are co-ordinates of the real world.

Godfrey Rust
October 2000

Breaking the chains

These poems were written between 1980 and 1991.

Poem for Christmas Eve (1988), *Joseph and the shepherds* (1989) and *Herod's last request* (1990) were written for carol services at St John's, West Ealing. *Peace, The word's out, Visitor* and *Breaking the chains* were originally commissioned for other events at St Johns.

Mr Gallup Reports is based on the results of a UK public opinion poll from the 1980s.

The professor at work and *The Flying Professor* were written for Colin Duckworth.

The Devil's Tinder Box was a name given to the Allied bombing of Dresden in February 1945.

Aberdaron is a village on the western tip of North Wales where the poet R S Thomas was once parish priest.

Laodicea (*A Laodicean estate agent writes*) is the church named in Revelation 3 as "lukewarm".

Adam

it wasn't me

it was that woman
she doesn't know what's good for her
she did it

and then
it was that snake
horrible slimy snake
I wouldn't have believed a word
I wouldn't have been taken in
imagine a talking snake
well I ask you

and then
and then
it was you
you made Eve
you made the serpent
it's your rotten apple
you knew all about it—
I was miles away
doing the garden like I was told

you're the one
you did it
it wasn't me
it *wasn't* me

and anyway I only took a little bite

Mischief

In the beginning
God made physicists
out of nothing at all.

"Now hold on,"
said the physicists,
"that's against a law."

God,
having not yet made Newton,
said nothing.

Then God made theologians
and became man
and joined them.

"Oh no," said the theologians,
"it's one thing or the other,
God or man."

God smiled
and passed the bread and wine.

Finally God made philosophers
and died for them.

"We've got you there,"
said the philosophers.
"Immortals don't die—it's inconsistent!"

But God,
having anticipated this objection,
got up,
packed away his shroud
and walked back into town to see his friends.

And then
just when he'd got them really interested,
just when then they were running out of arguments,
just when it looked like he'd put them straight
once and for all,
God made disciples
and left.

But that's God for you.
Always full of surprises.
Never know what he won't do next.
Wouldn't put it past him
just about now
with the physicists, theologians and philosophers
thinking they've almost worked it out
to come back
and prove them wrong again—

even though
it's the very last thing
he's likely to do.

Nuclear family

It wasn't so much a fall
as a fallout.
Eve split the apple
and started a Cain reaction
which no one was Abel to stop.

None has since escaped the sickness—
see how the children glow!
Beneath achievement's blossoming cloud
we measure out our half-lives,
radiant with sin.

The place where socks go

There's a place where socks go
    when the washing is done
and the driers have dried
    and the spinners have spun
and it's past eight o'clock
    and there's no one about
and the launderette's locked—
    then the odd socks come out.

There is hosiery here
    of each pattern and hue—
some plain, striped or spotted,
    some black, red or blue—
some worn only once,
    some so old they have formed
to exactly the shape
    of the foot they once warmed—

some were brought back from Sock Shops
    in airports in France,
some were hideous presents
    from matronly aunts—
but in all their variety
    one thing is shared:
to the place where socks go
    they will not go pre-paired.

Then the odd socks remaining
    are placed in the chest
(They must turn up sometime—
    now where was that vest...?)
and new socks come at Christmas
    and birthdays bring more
and the old lie, alone,
    at the back of the drawer.

And maybe, one evening
    when memory is low,
they too slip away
    to the place where socks go
and in silent reunion,
    each one with its pair,
they join in the dance
    with the other things there—

the letters unanswered,
    the calls not returned,
the promises broken,
    the lessons not learned,
the lost afternoons,
    the appointments unmade,
the best of intentions,
    the debts never paid,

and the friends not kept up
    and the others let down—
in the ragbag of conscience
    they waltz sadly round,
beyond the respite
    of the washing machine,
no amount of detergent
    can now get them clean

till that day when all laundry
    is washed white as snow,
and everyone's tumbled
    and soft soap must go,
when nothing is hidden
    but all is revealed
and socks shall be holy
    and souls shall be healed.

Revised version

Don't need my Bible any more.
I've got my daily paper.
They have so much in common.

On page 1
both name the Sun,
and differ only
on the identity
of the owner.

On page 2
both have strong opinions
on man's behaviour,
and differ only
(in the interests of fairness)
in that the serpent
is now given equal space
to put his view of things across,

and on page 3
both saw that they were naked,
and differ only now
in the fixed smiles
and the total collapse
of the fig-leaf market.

A modern wife

We grew up in the Sixties
when everything was new.
We only stopped at nothing
when nothing was taboo.
So who put up this barrier
that I cannot break through?

We had an open marriage.
We lived and we let live.
I never asked for anything
he didn't want to give.
So what is it we both resent
and neither can forgive?

We gave the kids their freedom
because it was their right.
They had the information.
They had the appetite.
So who is it I think I've failed
when they stay out all night?

We never hid our feelings.
We had no place for sham.
We freed ourselves to be ourselves.
We didn't give a damn.
So why is it I lie awake
and wonder who I am?

Joseph and the shepherds

Midnight in Bethlehem, Zero AD.
One or two people in difficulty.
Out on the street with a donkey and wife
Joseph had reached a bad point in his life
with the kind of a problem that won't go away:
a woman in labour, and nowhere to stay.
Now the root of it all, when you boiled the thing down,
was too many people in too small a town.
When they dreamed up the plan of administration
for a poll tax on all of the Jewish nation
only a bureaucrat somewhere like Rome
would send everyone back to their ancestors' home,
for little old Bethlehem wasn't designed
to cater for David's prolific line.
Still the problem was there and he couldn't disown it:
they'd left it too late, and Joseph had blown it.
If they'd finished the packing the evening before,
and not gone back to check that they'd locked the front
        door—
if they'd not missed the turning at that roundabout—
if they'd filled up the donkey before they set out—
if they hadn't agreed to call in and see
all of Mary's relations at Bethany—
or if only he'd booked by Israeli Express
that would have done nicely. But this was a mess.
No room at the inn. No room anywhere.
They gave him the only place they could spare
and the promised Messiah was born that night
on the floor of a stable without any light
where they cut the cord and cleaned up the mess
and wrapped him in somebody's workaday dress
and while Mary slept there, exhausted and cold,

Joseph sat by feeling helpless and old.
This wasn't the way he had thought it would be
when the angel had told him that destiny
chose them to look after the Holy One.
No, this was a farce. What God had done
was to trust the care of the Saviour instead
to a man who could not even find him a bed.
If only he'd planned it more carefully then.
If he only could go back and do it again.
He turned round in his mind the way he had
        blundered—
then he looked at the infant and suddenly wondered
if it all was a lie, if he was a fool
and the object of everyone's ridicule,
if the dreams of the angels were tricks and not
what they promised to be, and his anger grew hot
when the shepherds burst in all breathless and wild
and stopped in their tracks when they saw the child.
They shifted their gaze from the baby's bed
and their eyes met his, and he nodded his head,
standing awkwardly, not knowing quite what to do
now they all knew for certain the story was true.
They stayed there for minutes. It might have been years.
Not one of them spoke. Their hopes and their fears
were gathered around this helpless God
as their minds tried to grasp what it meant. Where he
        stood
Joseph was silent as finally
he saw this was how it was planned to be,
that the smell and the dark and the dirt and the pain
were not Joseph's mistake but God's choice. As the rain
ran down on Bethlehem Joseph knew

that men would be saved despite all they might do.
He could not control it. He did not understand.
He felt like a baby himself in God's hand.
He thought of his anger and flushed now with shame
He remembered the angel had said that his name
would be Jesus, God saves.
                  He glanced up and saw
that the shepherds had gone. Day had dawned. From
    the floor
Mary gazed at him, quizzical, on her straw bed.
The tiny God-child cried out to be fed.
Joseph moved to the business of the new day,
gave the child to its mother, the donkey some hay.

The appeal

Good evening. May I speak to you
about the little you can do
to contribute towards the health
of someone who can't help himself.
I'm sorry that it's such a bore.
You've seen them many times before—
these harrowing, pathetic scenes,
the faces on your tv screens
with staring eyes and hollow cheek
from playing squash three times a week.
Their diets bring them ever closer
anorexia nervosa,
their freezers swollen and distended—
this cannot be what God intended.
Their tap-water's undrinkable:
they buy Spa by the bottleful
and suffer quite beyond endurance
the ravages of health insurance.
They lack even the will to fight
the despot ruler, appetite,
or raise the least dissenting voice
against the tyranny of choice.
Pity those who can afford
the luxury of being bored.
This is the end of the appeal.
These problems are unbearable.
Send no money. What we need
is millions less mouths to feed.
Please carry on just where you're lying.
Don't let us interrupt your dying.

Roneo and Juliet

We met in the
Xerox copy shop,
each looking for
enlargements.
Her face
was my type
and I hoped she might
duplicate
my feelings,
but while I had it down
in black and white
it soon became transparent
she brought only
a handful of
negatives,

so seeing
there could be no
developments
I left,
wondering if
some day her
prints will come
prints will come
prints will come
prints will come
prints will come

Eve

Every time
    I get to the bit
  where the serpent

                                                sidles up to Eve
    telling the most blatant lie

I always think
    This time she won't fall for it
                not this time
                not our Eve

and every time
    I get to the bit
  where she takes the fruit
    (turning it lovingly in her artless fingers,
                stomach hollow with desire)

I always think
    DON'T DO IT
                surely this time she won't do it
but she does

every time, damn it
she does

Miracles

I don't believe in miracles.
There's always a rational explanation.

I believe
the Red Sea
was parted by a rockslide
coming at a convenient time
(though not convenient of course
if you happened to be Egyptian).

The five thousand were fed
by long French loaves
which they had selfishly
hidden up their jumpers
and which the Gospel writers carelessly
omitted to mention.

The water wasn't turned into wine exactly,
it was more God's way of saying
Water's very nice too, you know.

The healings weren't anything remarkable.
Jesus was just a good doctor
a bit ahead of his time,
say about 10,000 years.

As for the Virgin Birth,
I've always thought
that sort of thing just
inconceivable,

and Jesus didn't really rise.
His disciples just wanted
to keep the truth alive,
so they stole the body
and lied about it.

I don't believe in miracles.
There's always a rational explanation.

Riots by Reebok, blood by Benetton

The young today
have one parent,
two pairs of trainers
and a three-second attention span.

Sorry, did you miss that?

The young are consumers
of sex, television and hamburgers,
sometimes, for convenience,
all at the same time.

They think the world
owes them a living.
Unfortunately
it is seriously overdrawn.

The young don't know they're born.
So they keep fighting to get out.

The young have got it made.
So all they can do now
is take it to pieces again.

Don't be afraid of them.
They're only living
up to the expectations
in which they were raised.

The young today
have the world at their feet,
so they kick its brains out
in fits of designer rage,

missing parts easily replaced
at any branch of Body Shop.

The optimist explains

Of course
we must do
everything we can
to keep people alive

so that one day
someone may find out
why
we must do
everything we can
to keep people alive

The journey of the Magi (cont.)

Coming as they did from the first century
they had a few problems with London traffic
and were seriously misled by signs
to the Angel and King's Cross.

Inquiring diligently about the star
they were referred to Patrick Moore,
who hadn't actually seen God
but would keep an extra eyebrow raised.

In Harrods the camels
made a mess all over soft furnishings.
On the Underground
commuters glared at *No Smoking* signs
as incense wafted gently through the carriages.

And when the great day came
they saw the entire voting population
slumped on sofas by four o'clock,
rendered senseless by too much
dead poultry and the Queen,
while over Liberty's and Hamley's
the flickering angels sang
Glory to God in the High St...

...and they found him
(with the inns full up again)
in the old familiar place,
bringing their unregarded gifts
to the empty stable of the human heart
where the infant Christ is born
again and again and again.

Synod

The atmosphere was generous,
the speeches made with care,
the viewpoints all were fully heard,
the vote was free and fair,

and outside in the corridor
God waited patiently
to find that he existed
by a clear majority.

The dangers of theology

Where the apostles (fortunate of men
to understand your mysteries!) had then
only you, Holy Spirit, to draw on
we have concordance and the lexicon,
such commentaries and textual critiques
that keep our curates occupied for weeks
as verse by verse they plumb divinity.
The angels, awed, stand dumbly by as we
religiously apply the apparatus
(each new translation failing to placate us),
prod at your secrets, first this way then that,
as schoolchildren dissect a classroom rat
until Atonement dies before our pens
like blood under a microscopic lens
and Love, before which once we dared not speak,
becomes a mistranslation from the Greek.

Lord, all your gifts are worthy, and forbid
that fruits of scholarship should be kept hid,
but subtle is the pathway to disaster
when all the scholar's study is his master.
O thou who prayed to keep us from temptation
save us now from our imagination
lest—thinking in our ingenuity
it's *you* who falls beneath *our* scrutiny—
we file and reference till we can recall
only the doctrine, not the All-in-All
and let you Lord (it will not save our necks)
be crucified again, by card index.

Signs

By the traffic lights
the Indian grocer
promises FOO   VALUE
while over Piccadilly
the red and white neon
of the Coke sign insists
It's the Real Th g
to Eros' downturned stony face.

People are so casual
you'd almost think
it was a matter of
complete indifference
whether or not
you understood things
they have to say,
things like
 ake the plung
and
I th nk
I ove
yo

Arithmetic

That you and I are one is surely true,
yet just as plainly you and I are two,

and now you say (on looking in your heart)
that you against yourself take your own part

and being both the judge and advocate
this civil strife further divides our state—

a fractioning which scarcely makes us three,
for I can see the selfsame thing in me.

So with a schizophrenic sense I draw
this obvious conclusion: we are four.

Small wonder if in heaven there's consternation
at this quadratic amorous equation—

the Lord above is only One-in-Three,
but both of you is one with both of me.

The professor at work

The professor is painting his gate.
    As the sun warms the ground
    the only slight sounds
are the swishes his brush-strokes create.
It is early, some time before eight.
    While his wife slumbers on
    and unhelped by his son
the professor is painting his gate.

The marking of papers must wait.
    Though the act may inflame
    his detractors, who claim
the department is in quite a state
and the standard to which they translate
    the works of Hugo
    is appallingly low,
the professor is painting his gate.

His writings may well fascinate
    but the proofs lie unread
    by the side of his bed
and his critics, still insatiate,
merely sharpen their pencils and wait—
    while the world remains vague
    on the *Life of d'Antraigues*
the professor is painting his gate.

What becomes of the culture he taught?
    Now the philistine hordes
    are down-treading the boards
has the battle that so long was fought
now been lost? Has the thing become sport?
    Let his colleagues demur—
    alors, le professeur
est en train de peindre sa porte.

Some have said he may one day be great,
    that his restless *esprit*
    courts a rare destiny,
but for now this appointment with fate
is postponed until some future date,
    while the name that lifts eyebrows
    on many French highbrows
is quietly painting his gate.

Now he stops, and his back becomes straight.
    He steps back a pace
    and a smile splits his face.
There is nobody near to ovate
but with pleasure quite commensurate
    with achieving the peak
    of *palmes académiques*
the professor has finished his gate.

Philosophy

In the unweeded garden of the heart
the dog Philosophy goes
and he wonders if this is a foxglove
and he wonders if this is a rose
and he marks out his patch O so carefully
and the stench goes right up his nose
and he buries his bones and he digs them all up
and he wonders why none of them grows

Mr Gallup reports

Now that truth is a matter of opinion
we took a poll
to find out what we should believe in.

Reincarnation (27 per cent)
has hit a low point,
but it'll be back.

Satan (30 per cent)
is said to be quietly satisfied
but hopes to do worse next time.
In his opinion
it's better the Devil you don't know
as what you don't know can't hurt you, can it?

Heaven (57 per cent)
sure beats the hell out of
Hell (27 per cent),
a triumph of hope
over experience.

Sin (69 per cent)
despite the best efforts
of social work and education
is sorry to be still so obvious
and after all this time so unoriginal,

while God (76 per cent)
tops the poll
and wonders that so many still believe
yet never bother
to let him know

The man who got on at Ealing

The man
    who got on at Ealing
        talks to strangers. He says

Meaning is
    a function of a discourse situation.
        The leg of his spectacles

is held in place with Sellotape.
    He knew a mathematician called
        Reifenberg, or was it

Reisenberg? The name
    was lost in the tunnel's
        din; in any case

he's dead now, poor chap,
    fell off a mountain in the Dolomites,
        but he could drop his prejudices

instantly, like the man who got on at Ealing
    seeking a mathematical foundation
        for language, his manuscript

sitting in a stranger's lap,
    about to drop a
        bombshell on an unsuspecting world

before the man
    who got on at Ealing Broadway
        gets off.

Squiggles

Maybe God's at home in heaven today.
The sun seems to smile down,
doling out warmth and light
as if just for us.

But we know better.
The sun
is quite indifferent to our welfare
and wouldn't be the least concerned
if the world were under permafrost,
or reduced to a small glowing cinder
following a neutron attack
by nine-foot aliens from the planet Zog.

The sun has quite enough problems of its own,
such as dealing with spots
like any other adolescent star,
and wondering how to get itself a tan.

Yet long ago,
when the human race was in its early laps,
things seemed to be heaven sent.
Sun was a god
riding his chariot across the sky.
Thunder and lightning kept us on our toes.
Stars knew their place.
The moon was lit conveniently most nights.

Then science got down to it—
a private eye digging for dirt,
to prove that his client
had been seriously deceived.

And now
after extensive research
in the features section of *The Guardian*
and the first eight pages of
A Brief History of Time
I can reveal the origins of life itself,
which is to do with
squiggles.

What happened was
15 billion years ago
something went bang
(or maybe more of a whump,
we're still working on that bit)

and the squiggles set off
across whatever was there at the time
to begin the becoming
or become the beginning.

The squiggles spread
and all things being equal would have turned
into a kind of cosmic goo
like Chinese restaurant chicken & sweetcorn soup
without the sweetcorn.

But there were little ripples
like noodles in the soup
which pulled the squiggles
into lumps
and then turned into bits
of things.

Waiter
there's a squiggle in my soup.
Never mind sir
just leave it there long enough
it'll evolve into a fly—
but only if conditions
are favourable.

The other planets didn't have what it takes.
Mercury flew close to the sun
but forgot to revolve
and so it roasts itself on one side
like an abandoned beefburger on a barbecue.

Venus took the leisure centre approach
but someone must have left the sauna on
for a few billennia

and conditions on Jupiter
have clearly depressed
the market for timeshares,

but evolution,
like Goldilocks
trying out all the possibilities,
found one place that was just right—

it seems that
of all the planets
in all the solar systems
in all the universe
we had to squiggle into this one.

Of course
we may not be alone.
But if there is life elsewhere
it may not be as we know it.

Perhaps elsewhere a squiggle
became a squoggle
and so people on another planet
have three heads and one foot
and Carry On films are there considered
the highest form of culture.

Meanwhile back on earth
the squiggles became hieroglyphics
then an alphabet
and finally a digital display
on the screen of the ultimate laptop
working out its view of life
as a series of mathematical equations.

The gaps in which God might be found
are closed up daily.

The tabloids report he was last seen
clothed in a tatty sentimentality
skulking in the doorway of a West End church
cadging coppers from old ladies.

The laptop says
the board of superstition
has been swept clean—

prayers are no more use than touching wood,
demons are now exercised by drugs,
drought is caused not by divine judgement
but by bad management—
cosmic blame can now be laid squarely at the door
of the Anglian Water Authority

and though horoscopes are still quite interesting
it seems that God didn't make
the little green apples,
rainbows are just a trick of the light,
the Man's no longer in the Moon,
our feelings are just nerves following the brain's agenda
and words are only noises that we make.

The program writes itself out
towards the Superlaw,
the single, ultimate equation
and as for other explanations
they are just stories,
and stories can't be true
because they can't be proved

and so our dream is that one day
Winnie-the-Pooh will stump off up the forest
to discover the defective gene
which will account for Eeyore,
the wolf will put Red Riding Hood away for ever
and Father Christmas, Jesus and the fairies
will go to Never-Never Land
where they will find security of tenure
in the Department of Psychology

and we shall read our children bedtime algebra,
softly crooning quantum lullabies
as they drift off into the black hole of sleep.

But in their dreams
the theories unravel—

Darwin had a good shot with evolution,
but if only the fittest survive
what can explain the continuing existence
of Spud-U-Like and Barry Manilow?

The hypothesis
that we live in just one
of an infinite number of universes
is surely nothing more than comfort
for Scottish football fans
that somewhere, sometime
they must have qualified for a semi-final,

and if this is the best
of all possible worlds,
then what is Milton Keynes?

The results have come back from the lab
but they're rather disappointing.
Perhaps there's been some kind of mix-up—

is a photograph really no more than black dots?
Is music just a stream of data?
Is a diamond nothing more
than a seriously depressed piece of carbon,

or a kiss only a comprehensive exchange of germs?
Is metaphor coincidence
and art just fashion,
blood a useful carrier of nutrients,
sweat a consequence of overheating
tears an involuntary chemical reaction
caused frequently by death,
which itself is only the molecules
no longer vibrating?

The equations say
that these words here on this page
are nothing more than squiggles.

It seems we have
some work still to do on all this.
Grant applications are pouring in
for more research into the structure
of truth goodness beauty love and evil,
why Keats didn't just write
Ode On a Grecian Squiggle
or Shakespeare pen
All's Well That Ends In Squiggles.

The mathematics strain to look
over their shoulder to see
who it might be
who turns the dots back into pictures
and noises into music.

Where can we find him?
After we've taken the universe apart
and looked under every piece
of cold, dark matter
and pronounced him missing
(or at least that he's been in a meeting
for a very long time)

will we hear him
walking in the garden of genetics
in the cool of the universe's day?

Or see him
gazing out at us
from the cold, dark matter of the heart
which is not located by telescopes
or susceptible to chemotherapy?

We may well have been fooled,
like the deconstructionist English student
who took his word-processor to pieces
to find the meaning of the poem he'd just written,

and what then if
the point he's really making
as he writes out his universe in its endless
tantalising, well-designed equations
is just one simple, massive overstatement:

Look at it—
and none of this is of as much value
as the soul that your technology will never find!

Now will you believe me
when I tell you
just how much you are worth?

This boy curled up on his father's knee
draws squiggles with a felt-tip pen,
coaxing them into significance.
Upon the paper
they turn into a park, a car, a street

and this girl on her garden swing
makes quantum jumps onto the lawn
grinning in a wholly uncalculated way

and above
the sun seems to smile down,
doling out warmth and light
as if just for us.
Maybe God's at home in heaven today.

Four truths

The poorest truth is logical.
Picks its way through stumbling blocks.
When it meets a paradox
bangs its head against a wall.

The second is poetical.
Steps aside where logic sticks.
Swaps around the building bricks.
Has no plan to it at all.

The third is metaphorical,
the most that we can understand,
snapshots of the promised land.
Jesus chose the parable.

The last truth is the best of all:
purpose yet to be revealed,
paradox to be unsealed.
This will take the curtain call.

Apocalypso

In the night while we slept
the bombs fell on Tripoli
and up in the Four Horsemen's stables
the grooms lay awake

wondering if this was another fire drill
or if this was the real thing at last.

The comfort of the rain

Pentecost Sunday,
June Nineteen-Ninety,

and the world hasn't yet
blown its fatal hole in the ozone layer.

Jesus is further delayed
for reasons not fully stated:

the extra nineteen hundred years
have left us time to study eschatology

and learn the meaning of 'the time is short'
which Paul could not have known. Tonight

across the city in a thousand churches
hands will be raised

to a hundred thousand slightly different Gods,
and voices will call down the Spirit's fire

as they called to Baal on Carmel.
But there is no Elijah, no Simon Peter,

no tongue of flame on the wet branches
in this almost empty park, only these last few children

who swing through arcs of gravity,
who spin on the axis of this roundabout

feeling the pull of nameless forces
and the comfort of the rain.

Herod's last request

When Herod came to dinner we
locked up the silver cutlery—
though king of God's own chosen nation
he had a certain reputation.
Quite a few later remarked
on how his chariot was parked:
it didn't really do much harm,
just set off the odd car alarm
(and anyway they never use
wing-mirrors on BMWs).
One thing we were grateful for—
his guards remained outside the door.
They said they didn't mind it snowing
and whiled away the time by throwing
javelins at next door's cat
(the neighbour's curtains twitched at that).
We set an extra place or two
for the Ethiopian eunuchs who
he brought along to taste his food.
I said his timing's very good,
dropping by on Christmas Day:
we were entertaining anyway.
Herod chewed the turkey fat
and chatted about this and that—
the cost of temple services,
the relative advantages
of burnt offerings over frankincense—
we seemed to have his confidence
and in a weak, unguarded minute
(just like me to drop us in it)
I brought up, casually aside,
the subject of infanticide.

Remembering John the Baptist's head
I was concerned at what I'd said
but then we saw, to our surprise,
a twinkle came in Herod's eyes.
"Why, don't you know what brought me here?
Well, then I must make it clear!
I've come to pay my compliments
to fellows with a common sense.
Say, don't you think that we might be
in the same business, you and me?
I kill by violence, you neglect—
and here you've earned my deep respect
for I can only be selective:
your methods are much more effective.
Just let an open sewer stink,
give him no clean water to drink
or basic medical supplies
and see how quickly one child dies!
By careful acts of selfishness
you have created such a mess
you now eliminate about—"
(he took his calculator out)
"—forty thousand every day."
He smiled and put the thing away.
"You can destroy whole continents
simply by indifference.
But though I like what you don't do,
your actions are impressive too.
You take the mineral resource,
the inexpensive labour force,
most of the profits they can earn
and then you leave them in return

Coca-Cola and Big Mac,
debts they never can pay back,
spare change you feel good in giving,
cardboard packaging to live in.
A hundred million children now
sleep on the planet's streets somehow
apprenticed into useful trades
like prostitution, drugs and AIDS—
though I'm both cruel and sadistic
I can't compete with that statistic,
nor with the armaments I know
you've built to keep the status quo.
I just had swords and knives and spears
but after nineteen hundred years
you have such powerful weapons
their cost alone kills millions!
However population climbs
you can destroy it fifty times
and fight it on a dozen fronts
while you don't feed it even once.
That's big league stuff compared to me
who butchers a baby boy (or three).
There's nothing more I need to do—
I'll leave my murdering to you.
A toast is called for now, I think.
This Christmas evening let us drink
to all the damage that's been done
by looking after Number One!"
He raised his glass up to his head—
the wine it held was rich and red—
and looking round from face to face
he said "But we should say a grace!

Give thanks to those in direst need
who starve so we can overfeed
and die to do us sinners good.
We eat their flesh and drink their blood.
Do this, as oft as you remember,
at least once every December."
Then Herod laughed, and drained his wine.
Somehow I couldn't stomach mine,
yet though he smiled, his eyes were grim—
something clearly unsettled him.
"I murdered boys aged two or less,
and this was done under duress.
If you should want to place the blame
then put the Magi in the frame:
if I had not been so deceived
by those wise men, then I believe
much blood would never have been spilled.
I only needed one child killed.
My motive was quite rational:
stability in Israel
depends on keeping sweet somehow
whoever's emperor just now.
This story of a new-born king
could only be unsettling:
he was a danger, patently,
to national security
and threatened also therewithal
my throne, my life, my soul, my all.
So—proving that my word is good—
I went just as I said I would
to worship at his incarnation.
He had my total dedication.

Everything was sacrificed
until I found the baby Christ.
And did you think I'd failed? Oh, no.
Though it took thirty years or so
my people got the brat at last
and strung him up and held him fast
and made quite sure that he was dead.
And there he should have stayed. Instead
something went wrong. I don't know how,
I just know he is not dead now
and like a nightmare in my brain
it happens time and time again—
with lives for stables, hearts for mangers,
he is born to total strangers
and so I cannot rest secure
until the child is found once more
and the botched work of Calvary
is completed finally.
That's why I'm here, and why I stay,
for now a billion times a day
those nails are hammered deeper in
by each act of your human sin
and, though each time the God man dies
somehow he manages to rise,
still there may—I don't despair—
evil enough to hold him there.
If Christ is born again in you
is he not often murdered too?
Surely someone hates enough
to overcome this power of love?
I depend on, you, you see.
Please, finish off this job for me."

Convert

He came to
faith in
All Souls,
but it wasn't
until much later
that finally
he came to
faith in
all circumstances.

Disciple

I will follow you.

I will go to the ends of the earth for you
so long as the earth is round.

I will die to the flesh
in the sure and certain hope of resurrection.

I will put away the old man
for safe keeping.

Your yoke is easy—
that's good.
I don't mind what it costs
if I can afford it.

I don't mind doing my bit on the cross.
We could have a rota.
Put me down for a couple of hours
Sunday evening

and please don't use nails.

I will follow you
carefully,
with helpful advice.

I will follow you
wherever I want to go.

Peace

We may say *It is peaceful*,
but this is not peace.
This is just the absence of noise.
Somewhere noise goes on—
in the ambulance sirens,
in the sweat-shops in Hong Kong,
in the veins of the addict,
in the minds of the wrongly-imprisoned
and the mother of the cot-death baby
the noise goes on but we don't hear it.
Our ears are plugged
with the wax of self-importance
so we say *It is peaceful*,
but it is not God's peace.
This is the peace the world gives
and its real name is pride.

We may say *We live at peace*,
but this is not peace.
This is just the absence of war.
Somewhere war goes on—
in parts of America,
through half of Asia,
across most of Africa,
in the shopping centres of Ulster
and the litter bins of London
the war goes on but we don't see it.
We have turned our eyes away
because it won't happen here,
so we say *We live at peace*,
but it is not God's peace.

This is the peace the world gives
and its real name is indifference.

We may say *Now, he is at peace*,
but this is not peace.
This is just the absence of life.
Somewhere life goes on—
in the house he never owned,
in the job he almost finished,
in the children he meant to talk to,
in the wife he failed to love,
in the father he couldn't remember
and the mother he wouldn't forgive
life goes on but he doesn't live it,
so we say *Now, he is at peace*,
but it is not God's peace.
This is the peace the world gives
and its real name is death.

The peace of God
is nothing like this.
It is more like noise.
It is more like war.
It is more like life.

The peace of God
is like the peace of the tightrope walker
balancing a hundred feet above Niagara Falls.

It is in the peace of the cancer patient
for whom treatment is no longer prescribed.

It is in the peace
in the quiet moment
after the fatal road accident.

It is in the peace
of a ruined, liberated city.

It is in the peace
at the centre of the whirlwind
that tears the island to pieces.

It is in the peace
at the opening of the gates
of Auschwitz.

It is the peace of the man
who has lost everything
so has nothing else to lose.

It is the peace of Stephen
as the first stones bruise his body.

It is the peace of Gethsemane,
saying *Nevertheless your will be done.*

It is the peace of the carpenter
as he steadies his hammer
for the last blow on the nail.

It is the peace of the women
on their necessary business
in the desolate dawn.

At Grasmere

The blue-
black mayfly danced
for half a minute
by my shoe.

Tessa was glad.
"How sad
to live for a day
if nobody knew".

Drunkard

When first it was offered
a drop was enough—
you weren't even sure
that you liked the stuff,

but you were quite young
and your palate was chaste—
with some perseverance
you soon got the taste.

You could take it or leave it?
That's what they all think.
Soon your only desire
was for just one more drink.

Now it's straight from the bottle,
not even a cup,
and you splutter and hiccup
and bring it back up

and bloated and bleary
you lurch into bed,
not one ounce of remorse
in your stupefied head.

Well you're satisfied now
but you don't know till when,
and first thing in the morning
you're at it again—

it's not whisky or gin
(who on earth would drink that!):
it's the thin white warm hard stuff
that lays you out flat—

you may sleep through the night
and you don't suffer colic
but, baby, you know
you're a real milkaholic.

Nappy Christmas

Awash in a manger
the baby awakes

we didn't buy Pampers
we all make mistakes

The housewife's evening prayer

I hope I'll go to heaven
but I'd like to know one thing:
in the Father's many mansions
who does the hoovering?

I'd love to join the feasting
and drink the bridegroom's cup,
but could you reassure me
about the washing up?

Are the angels' haloes polished?
Do their tunics fit alright?
And do any little cherubs
need a bottle in the night?

Of course I'm sure that everything
we do there will be nice,
but absolutely *nothing*
would make it paradise.

Poem for Christmas Eve

This is a love story, if you can accept it,
that God the father looked down at his world
and the world was like a sleeping, fitful child
and the child was spoiled.

Its nations called each other names
and roamed earth's playground like a gang of boys
who choose sides, always brandishing
their terrifying toys.

The world thought it was fatherless and hunted
restlessly for some new sign or token
as if Christmas had come and gone, its presents all
unwrapped, already broken,

and the father God looked at his child
and counted the cost of love's freedom: but he had a
    plan,
to step from out of time and into history
and become a man.

With eternity to find the spot he chose
with the greatest care. One night a workman stood
in a barn with a group of animals
watching the birth of God

while out on the hills some shepherds were astonished
as a skyful of angels appeared then disappeared,
and a few astrologers saw a change in the stars
they'd studied for years

and almost everyone else knew nothing.
Caesar turned and settled in his luxurious bed
while in Bethlehem the power and the glory
bawled for milk in a shed.

It was quite an entrance. The only Son of God
homeless, illegitimate, a refugee,
owning nothing but the world that he grew up in
had made himself quite empty,

his birth itself a kind of dying where
he abdicated power, omniscience,
was needy, hated and misunderstood
and after the last violence

would be laid in the womb of a grave for the birth
which Bethlehem merely anticipated
and for which the blind, brave, barricaded
spoiled world waited—

no sage or rustic coming there with gifts,
only some women, hopelessly brave,
bringing spices in the dark of morning
to an empty grave.

Two deaths, two births, the manger and the cross:
the first brought hope, the second brought salvation.
Out of his poverty this child has made us rich
beyond imagination,

and on a winter evening in a London home
a father looks down at his sleeping child.
The room is warm and brightly lit. Outside
the night is darkly wild,

and the child that sleeps knows well that she is loved,
and in her bones knows how to disobey,
and she will learn that none is innocent,
that death takes all away,

and the father looking at her peaceful face
feels his own helplessness and counts the cost
of the love between them in a spoiled world
where all must end in loss

but for Bethlehem and Calvary. These births
have brought an end to death,
and the child in the manger is the Lord
we feed on in our hearts by faith

now and forever. Child, if you would wake
on this Christmas Eve outside you'd find
a star, not a streetlamp. Listen, you can hear
the angels' message in the wind.

Monster

We don't know the planet
the monster came from, only that

it is here now and cannot return.
The keepers are not sure if it is harmful.

It is like a chameleon or a spaceman
(it has pointed ears—perhaps it was on Star Trek).

They prod it to make sure it's still alive.
The monster stirs. Its face

is nearly recognisable. The keepers feed it
as much as they are able, and sometimes

the monster seems to humour them until
they almost think it may be tamed—but then

the monster roars and will not be consoled.
The keepers watch it, knowing now

they cannot penetrate its private grief,
and fear the wordless rage that tortures it. At night

it is kept behind bars for its own protection.
They try to make it comfortable.

The monster smiles. The keepers both relax,
rocking it into a milky sleep.

Told you so

Obedient to the latest thinking
of the *Sunday Times* medical experts
we raise the head of Emma's cot
two inches off the ground
with *The Pelican Guide*
to English Literature
under one leg
balanced up with
Keats' Collected Works.

Now I sleep doubly secure
knowing my daughter
will safely breathe,
and reassured in my belief
that poetry can make
the difference
between life
and death
after all.

Vocation

Others built cities,
crossed continents
and changed history.

He built sentences,
crossed t's
and changed typefaces.

He said God
why did it have to be words?
And God said

In the beginning
consider the cost
of my silence.

Beirut

When all this trouble started
I wrote a poem about you, Beirut.
It took me a very long time.
It was done with the utmost sensitivity.

You weren't grateful.
Politicians on all sides denounced it.
Militias ignored it.
Despite the support of many Western governments
the poem never had a chance.
Olive-skinned fanatics
with immaculate moustaches
told American newscasts
they would never recognise the poem
and all the time
plotted its annihilation.

When I finally got through to the poem
I could hardly recognise it myself.
Not a stanza was intact.
Shelling had been especially heavy
around the adjectives.
The bloody words just lay there
pleading for their pathetic lives.

It was over in seconds.
I hit the wastebin
rat a tat tat
without a ricochet.

Ben Franklin

When
in 1751
Ben Franklin
found out how lightning worked

cathedrals everywhere
put up conductors
to deflect thunderbolts
from heaven.

Another weapon gone
in the fight against heresy
sighed God,
changing tactics yet again.

The Devil's Tinder Box

He killed people. He was no more
than a boy, flying in a box with wings.

Four times the box went down, each time
with another crew up and so

he missed becoming a statistic and survived
to spend his life working statistics out.

The simple honesty which later marked
his handling of business affairs

would have been with him then: he must have killed
reluctantly but well. I only heard him talk

once about his thirteenth mission, on
February Thirteenth—he said

if ever his number was up
that should have been it; but by 1945

even daylight raids were almost unopposed—
with the Luftwaffe beaten they bombed more or less at
    will.

The dilemma that he faced was exquisite:
to do his job well, as he knew he must,

meant killing ever more effectively
those who were neither enemies nor friends,

whose weakness robbed the fliers of all excuses
but that they followed orders (the defence

that wouldn't serve at Nuremburg). On the
night of the Devil's Tinder Box

they knew what they were doing. The target,
all but unguarded, had no strategic value

but its railway, and was swelled with refugees
from Stalin's push west. *Poor bastards*, he said

all those years later, in a voice
I had never heard before. With the war already won

Dresden was still beautiful as my father
settled in the belly of the plane,

a wheel-hub (all bomb-aimers did this)
shielding his private parts from the chance caress

of a lucky shell from the untrained
flak guns of the terrified men below.

They had no credit cards

They had no credit cards said the manager
They could have been anyone

Sheep must be protected said the bishop
They're so easily upset

It's a vicious little province said the governor
You can't make allowances

How could we have known who it was
Tell us how we could have known

Because it's always me said the dead man
Tricky isn't it, it's always me

Body odour

This man whose arms are raised in prayer
exalts his Lord above the skies.
The Spirit rules him while he's here.
His wife controls him otherwise.

This woman prays with feeling for
the missionaries in Peru
while managing to quite ignore
the others sitting in the pew,

and this man, when the ritual's done,
wonders why it is that those
who are the fragrance of the Son
so often just get up his nose.

He lets all kinds of people in.
Here is your mother, sister, brother.
We eat and drink the stuff of sin.
This is the church. There is no other.

A Laodicean estate agent writes

The developers have moved in
on 1 Corinthians 13
(a delightful period chapter
retaining many of its original features)

The structural survey found Faith, Hope and Love
inadequate for modern requirements

The valuers found
that it profited them nothing

The planning office saw
as in a glass, darkly

The architect
believed all things

The contractor
hoped all things

The neighbours
endured all things

The builders
spoke with tongues of men
and definitely not angels

and now it's done and back on the market
these three remain
Ambition, Fear and Need

and the greatest of these
is never satisfied

You can't be too careful

The old lady
in the pew behind
exchanged the peace with me

but went up for Communion
clutching her handbag
just in case

Notes for a biography

When Jesus went to Bethlehem
I must say it was odd—
I wouldn't have been born that way
if I was being God.

When Jesus went to Nazareth
he spent twenty years in trade—
that's hardly a career
in which Messiahs will be made.

When Jesus picked his followers
a practised eye could tell
he was plainly inexperienced
at hiring personnel.

When Jesus wandered Palestine
it was awfully hit and miss—
you'll never reach your customers
with marketing like this.

When Jesus worked a miracle
you don't need a degree
to know that healing on the sabbath
will annoy a Pharisee.

When he went to Jerusalem
he rode there on an ass—
what a PR opportunity
and Jesus let it pass.

When he went to Gethsemane
the game was not yet up—
there was time for him and Judas
to kiss and make it up.

When Jesus stood in Pilate's house
he didn't realise
that politics is all about
the art of compromise.

When Jesus went to Calvary
that's the ending of the story —
one more tragic hero,
death instead of glory.

He must have been mad
that's the only way I understand it—
when Jesus went to Calvary
you'd almost think he'd planned it.

Dream

Woke before the alarm. Pulled
the covers over my head
but you can't avoid the day for ever. Outside
the windscreen was white with frost. Poured
a kettleful of water over it and drove
squinting through the frozen rivulets.

                                        One theory is
dreams are the way that the unconscious mind
sorts the day's debris, like a berserk computer—
fear, loss, guilt, desire, the girl in the mirror
at the traffic lights, in dark glasses ... how is it
I never dream about you, God?

Aberdaron

We may suppose he has been here. There is
evidence: this bay, this headland,

the clouds' endless commentary
as if to say *See what was done*

with one word, and so many millennia.
We must suppose it. Nothing

else will free the hung jury of our reason,
like a child in a game

counting to ten, to a hundred, a thousand—
Ready or not, here I come! Silence

and the shadow of a gull's wing on the water,
the slow breaking of the sea.

The word's out

Sometimes
I listen for your word
and hear nothing.

In the quiet of my room
the only noise
is the thump of my own heart
and angry voices arguing in my head.

You can't say I don't give you a chance.
Sometimes I may say nothing
for as long as five minutes.
Your silence is still deafening.

But then I open a book
and out tumbles your voice.
And when I try to shut that up
I find you can get a word in anywhere.

I've even heard you sometimes from the pulpit.

I hear you on the Nine O'Clock News
saying "What have you done
with the world I gave you?"

I hear you in the tabloids
saying "Whoever is without sin
cast the first stone."

With the first burst of spring flowers
you say "Look—no hands!"

With the most extraordinary sunset
you say "Look, just relax".

The shrunken face of hunger
is you saying "Feed me".

The beggar on the underground
is you saying "House me".

The dreaded diagnosis
is you saying "Heal me".

The valium prescription
is you saying "Free me".

The redundancy notice
is you saying "Value me".

The scream of the torture victim
is you saying "Father, forgive".

The priest staring down the barrel of a gun
is you saying "Love casts out fear".

When I am late and hurrying
you are the face on the clock
saying "I am the beginning and the end".

When I am greedy
you are the face on the banknote
saying "Treasure is in heaven".

When I am proud
you drop your banana-skins in front of me
saying "Don't look down".

When I am lonely
you are the stillness of the house
saying "I am with you, always".

And when I am grieving
you are the voice at the graveside
saying "I am the Resurrection and the Life".

Sometimes
I listen for your word
and hear nothing.

And sometimes
you make so much noise
I can hear nothing else.

Home improvements

You can't trust anyone these days.
Take this Jesus.
Seemed OK. We asked him in,
just being neighbourly, the way you do.

Over dinner he was pleasant enough
apart from an annoying habit
of turning the small talk into conversation.
Even seemed keen to hear about
our plans for home improvements.
So we showed him round.

This was the big mistake.
When it came down to it
he wasn't really interested
in the kitchen units
or the bathroom tiles
or the artificial ceiling in the lounge,
but kept peering into cupboards uninvited
(as if we had dry rot)
and prizing up the edges of the carpet
(as if we had woodworm)

and finally disappeared into the cellar
(heaven knows what he found down there)
emerging with a hammer
and a pickaxe and a drill
and a pocketful of drawings
and smiling in a most alarming way said
I've just had a much better idea

and started smashing down the walls

Visitor

What is that rushing sound
where all has been so quiet?
Who howls around this house
making the blood run riot?

Who is it that he seeks?
What passion in him strains
that he should shake the doors
and crack the window panes?

What comfort will he bring
or anguish bring about?
What if we let him in?
We cannot keep him out—

it is the breath of God:
at Pentecost he came
there to embrace his love
in arms of leaping flame,

a cold and silent fire
that burns within the soul
until it is consumed
into the purest gold.

Phantom

The limb removed, the amputee
swears there's an itching
where hand or foot was,
a ghostly memory
of something once attached.

There are phantom people too.
It's unimportant, almost
nothing, just some trick
on eye and mind
of a slight, familiar imprint—

a motorway sign, a certain
tilt of a woman's head.

Runner

'We don't have a climate, only weather',
and plenty of it. Tessa

hates it, it keeps her inside. I put on
my rain-suit with the hood drawn fight and splash

seven or eight miles along the river,
my Nikes soaked through and half the Thames Basin

to wash off in the bathtub when I get back home.
You need to run on days like these

when the wind gusts force nine up the river
throwing the past at you in bucketsful

and even memory loses its nerve.
You need to outrun the ghosts

that crowd the river path under the trees
and brush like nettles as you race past,

these faces, hostages of the storm, lovers
and those who were never lovers

and someone once, a girl, a woman really,
I don't say I knew her well—those dreams

that are lies, such lies
they are better left in the rain on the darkening path

as I stand panting for breath outside my own front
    door.
I love my wife. My study is a tidy room

full of questions stacked on bricks and planks—
Knowing God, Sex in the Real World,

How to Manage Pressure, Running to Win—
which will stay unanswered for another six months

at which time the whole lot comes down
to make way for a cot and a baby,

and I will sit then
in the room at the back of the house

hearing this weather above my typewriter's clatter,
hearing the rainfall at the end of summer, drumming

on garden leaves in the cool of the evening
the endless whisper, *Love me more than these.*

The Flying Professor

When they're stacking for miles above Orly
and Heathrow is shrouded in fog
and the captain of many a grounded plane
makes an entry of gloom in his log,

when the seat reservation computer
has crashed and gone down with all hands
and the bags have been sent to Vancouver
when the labels said Grange-over-Sands,

to a seasoned air traffic controller
the reason is perfectly plain,
and the crews all exchange knowing glances—
the Professor is flying again!

In the queue at gate B27
in Melbourne or Bangkok or Rome
he is clutching his boarding card tightly
like the key to his second home,

and the faces all seem so familiar
as he settles down into his seat,
and they hand him the *Herald Tribune*
and they hand him a purple boiled sweet

and the widebodied 747
taxis off with immaculate care
till it charges headfirst down the runway
and climbs up to heaven knows where,

and while he's the first to acknowledge
that travel has broadened his mind
he suspects it of having an equal effect
on his waistline and on his behind,

so he presses the recline button
and kicks off his travelling shoes
and pulling the eyeshade down over his face
drifts off into sleep—well, a snooze—

and he's snug in his blow-up neck collar
with the plugs nestled tight in his ear
and the stewardess straightens his blanket
and whispers "Rest now, you poor dear…"

In the legends of aviation
a tragic new tale has begun,
as poignant as Icarus seeking
a weekend away in the sun—

it's the curse of the Flying Professor
condemned to stay up in the air
because half of his family lives over here
while the other half lives over there.

And sometimes, when changing at Frankfurt
or stopping for fuel in Bahrein,
his future life passes before him
in the form of a journey by plane.

Like a scene from a play by Sam Beckett
he is somewhere that's just in between,
writing pieces on shopping in Aix-la-Chapelle
for Aer Lingus in-flight magazine,

and he can't find the summoning button
as the stewardess flashes a smile,
and he's one seat away from the window
and he's one seat away from the aisle

tied up in an orange lifejacket
that will never completely inflate
while another light meal is served every half hour
and left, just out of reach, on a plate,

as they hit little pockets of turbulence
(you do on the smoothest of trips)
which come at precisely the moment
he lifts his full cup to his lips,

and the film is something from New Zealand
that has not reached the cinemas yet
and he can't seem to alter his headphones
which are tuned in to Tammy Wynette

and he quietly fingers his sick-bag
for he's not one for making a fuss
but perhaps it's the slight whiff of sulphur
that's making him so nauseous—

and he has an uneasy feeling
as the FASTEN YOUR SEATBELT sign warns
he could swear that the grinning attendant
was wearing a small pair of horns—

as the tyre-rubber burns on the runway
he knows there's as much of a chance
of his reaching the end of these wanderings
as Glenn Miller of landing in France,

and he's sure now he journeys in vain to escape
the conclusion he cannot resist:
if it's better to travel in hope than arrive
he's the world's number one optimist.

Carrick

In case Galilee proved a disappointment
this was the understudy,

the hillsides green and suitable for preaching,
the fishing good, sudden squalls

giving way to miraculous calms,
weather that, like Him, each day decides

whether to be wind or fiery sun,
earth tremor or the still and quiet voice.

First lesson

Peter at the cock-crow
Jonah in his fish

before you get the glory
it always comes to this

Economics

Here
is the only successful
planned free-market
in the history of the world,

where the cost of living
and the wages of sin
are the same

and the rate of exchange is fixed
at one life
given as a ransom
for many.

Has anybody here seen Thomas?

Sometimes I feel
like an Easter Saturday,
                           just
a tombful of possibilities
wishing my guard
would fall asleep.

Mary

And if you ask me what a Christian is
I'd say, not him who's pure in word and deed,
or goes to all the Sunday services,
or says his prayers, or knows the proper creed,

but that one who would gladly give away
all that he has now or has ever been
to stand between the dark tomb and the day
and know the moment of the Magdalene.

Breaking the chains

My first escape bid
came at the age of nought.
Nine months in mummy's tummy—
no more room in the womb.
So with the help of nothing
but two midwives,
one anxious father
and the best technology the NHS had to offer
(I've always been a gambler)
I made my dash for freedom,
lowering myself carefully
on the umbilical cord
ready for the big push.

I got caught.
They threw me in the crib
for six months solitary confinement,
then two years in the cot and playpen
with nappies off for good behaviour.

With native cunning I survived
playschool and nursery, but from then on
it was just one institution after another
until at eighteen
I came out from behind bars
and began leaning on them instead.

It soon became clear
my family was keeping me under house arrest.
My children
were born in captivity,

and then one day with a shock I found
I had been taken hostage.
I was held alone
in a small room
for seven to eight hours at a stretch
with the minimum of comfort—
a bare desk,
a swivel chair,
a secretary,
two telephones,
an American Express card
and five weeks holiday a year.

At weekends I got parole.
I began to look everywhere
for some hope of freedom.

I combed the Sunday papers
and collapsed exhausted
under the weight
of the supplements.

I bought a microwave
a dishwasher
and many labour-saving devices
but they just left me in a vacuum.

I asked my bank manager
but he could find no interest
in anything free.

I reached for it
in a love affair with no strings
and still got tangled up
when I pulled the other one.

Looking deep into my personal computer
I typed ESCAPE?
and it replied
UNSPECIFIED COMMAND OR FILENAME

I searched for it on a desert island
with only eight gramophone records
and Sue Lawley for company
but I got fed up being asked questions
so I got away
on a raft of unused Bibles left by previous castaways.

I opened negotiations with the Devil
who couldn't promise freedom as such
but offered some interesting terms.

By now I had worked out
where everyone else had gone wrong
in the past.
They had made the mistake
of dying,
so I trained my body and mind
not to be a slave to anything.

I nearly made it.
If I could just have controlled
a few small details

like my temper,
my sex drive,
my need to eat and drink
and my annoying habit of falling unconscious
for eight hours every day,
I'm sure I would have found freedom.

Finally I set out to look for it on the open road
in my XR3i GT soft-top Cabriolet
nought to sixty in 4.5 seconds
but I got stuck in traffic
in the Wandsworth one-way system,

so I dialled it up on my car phone
and I got its answering machine
I'M SORRY FREEDOM IS
NOT AVAILABLE AT THE MOMENT
PLEASE LEAVE A MESSAGE
AFTER THE ATONEMENT

I had run out of ideas.
Turning on my radio I realised
I was not alone.
Whole countries were trying to get out.
Eastern Europe had made a break for it
leaving the Iron Curtain on the latch
and just a few short range missiles for cover.

The USA
had built itself a space shuttle
but it only took six people at a time
and anyway it kept coming back.

The Soviet Union
in desperation
attempted to declare
independence from itself,

while Britain
just tried to tunnel its way out.

Nobody made it.
It was easy to be wise after the event—
with all that pent-up anger,
banged up in the world day after day,
slopping out into the seas and oceans,
living three or four to a house in intolerable conditions
with nothing to do all day but live and die
it just had to e x p l o d e

They rioted in the squares,
they lit fires in the rainforests,
they made holes in the roof.

It was as if they'd found out
that the prison was inside them
and they were held by chains
of pride and fear and death,

they were guilty but were hoping
that there might be some helpful miscarriage of justice,
and they were looking for a fresh alibi
when God came innocently by
disguised as a man

saying If the Son shall make you free
you shall be free

and they said Indeed
We don't like your kind coming in here
You're not a normal offender
You interfere with people

Take that they said
handing him a crown
And that they said
look we've had a little whip round for you

and they said
anything you say will be taken down
and used against you
and God said nothing
and it was taken down
and used against him

and here they said
is something we're really cross about.
It's our little way of saying
we blame our parents
we blame society
we blame somebody else
we blame you.
Here is your fixed penalty,
fixed to this wooden beam.

But they didn't know
that each nail they hammered
through his wrists and ankles
broke a link of the chain that bound them

and when he said
It is finished
and they shut him up
under maximum security
tightly wrapped
behind a stone
behind a seal
behind a guard
and dead
just to be on the safe side

after a little while
they heard him say
Here I am
I've found the way out
and come back for you

all charges against you have been dropped
you're free to go
and follow me
or else stay here
in the prison of yourself
if you're afraid of what it might be like
on the outside.

The chains are broken,
look, it's you who's holding them together.

Teddy bears

When we have set all this aside—
name, reputation, history—
it will not be for us to slide
into dull uniformity.

Heaven will not level down.
These things that we identify
as most emphatically our own
have less to do with you and me

than we can here imagine. They
stand to life as a cartoon,
mere toys of personality.
We shall forget them quite as soon

as a small child who suddenly
puts aside his teddy bears
and runs, quite unselfconsciously,
to greet his Father on the stairs.

The sailing of the ark

To A.C.

We that are bound by vows, and by Promotion,
With pomp of holy Sacrifice and rites,
To teach belief in good and still devotion,
To preach of Heaven's wonders and delights:
Yet when each of us in his own heart looks
He finds the God there far unlike his Books
Fulke Greville, 'Chorus of Priests'

As the heavens are higher than the earth,
so are my ways higher than your ways
and my thoughts than your thoughts.
Isaiah 55, 9

The sailing of the ark is a sequence of forty-five poems written over a period of four years from December 1987. It had its first public reading in Ealing in December 1991.

The sequence is in the form of a letter to a friend: I am grateful to Andrew for agreeing to let it be published unchanged.

The drawing of a crucifixion on page 153 is based on sketches of a wood and steel sculpture by Scilla Verney, made shortly before her death from cancer. It is reproduced by kind permission of her husband Stephen.

The style of the poems—a loose form of sonnet without rhyme or strict metre—was borrowed from the late New Zealand poet, James K Baxter.

The poem contains a number of quotations and references, biblical and otherwise. There is not space enough to acknowledge them all here, but a set of notes on the sonnets is available from Wordsout (free by email or please send sae).

1

Andrew, another year has stripped
the leaves, like misconceptions, from the trees;

the last page of the kitchen calendar
prepares to drop, announcing the advent

of that season when, according to good scholarship,
Jesus couldn't have been born. The resurrection

waits on the other side of winter, and in
this month that asks for no apologies

the winds of daily living have laid bare
the root and branches of our faith—what

is it that remains when it has shed
all that's deciduous, its stark wooden

outline raised against the backdrop of this grey,
late-century, turbulent post-Christian sky?

2

Well, Andrew, we've reached life's middle ground,
surprised we got this far without being

found out, and still wondering
what it is we're going to do when we grow up; yet

I'm here somehow with all the regular stuff—
job, wife, mortgage, bank statements and bills,

bathroom ceiling needing papering,
two children to be got to bed by eight—while

the man I might have been digs with his bare hands
in the ruins of a bombed-out house in Basra

or lies on the ground in Africa with ribs
like a birdcage stretched across with parchment

and staring eyes fixed, I think, on something other
than a choice of curtains and the current mortgage rate.

3

Balding, overweight, at night I plod
the roads of W5 and W13,

a three-mile token gesture of a run,
dreaming of perfect mortal fitness,

dreaming that round the edge of Walpole Park
I shall one day run and not grow weary.

Jesus kept fit by walking, I suppose—
he never had a desk job, or grew old. I can recall

the day you left All Souls I met your father,
slow and wrinkled, as became his age—

yet once I heard the wireless commentary
on the 1936 Olympic Final

with your dad leading for six hundred metres
then fading, Lovelock coming through to win.

4

It's a numbers game. Our worth is measured out
on sets of calibrated scales. I'm 38,

drive a 2.2 GLE with heated seats
and ran a marathon in 2 hours 49. They give me

umpty tumpty thousand pounds a year
for naming things and organising them,

formulating Numbers for the Beast.
Apocalyptic? No, you've seen the codes,

those neat black beast-marks, such an efficient system,
across our cereal packs, even in our Bibles—

God knows, Andrew, I'm helping to promote them!
What nonsense! Why, we even got his birthday
    wrong—

Christ who was born in 4 or 5 BC
laughs and weeps at us, his self-made ciphers.

5

At thirty-five thousand feet,
wearied of business, I looked out to see

the winter sun throw into sharp relief
a barren land of mountains, a fine show

of geology's inhumanity to man.
A drift of cloud had settled on Geneva

like a quilt thrown on a bed—what light or warmth
has the tiny match-flame of our creativity

against all this? Of course he made it,
just as he made the cold terrain of the psyche

or soul, or spirit, call it what you will,
with its unclimbed ridges and deeper valleys,

and some always in shadow, however high
the sun of righteousness rises on healing wings.

6

Some of our friends who came so earnestly
to those lectures and courses, they live now

with things we thought untenable—divorced,
or practising homosexuality, or they just gave it up,

finding that model of the Christian life
came to pieces in their hands, their hard-earned
     knowledge

icing failure with guilt. Was it sin?
Or faithlessness? Or was there also

a lack of power in that theology,
tried and exhausted by experience, its careful

applications weak appeasement to the deep
imperatives of our disordered minds and bodies,

waved like Chamberlain's fluttering paper—"Peace in
     our time"—
against the darker annexations of the human will?

7

The wind roared unannounced across
the reclaimed islands of the Ganges delta,

dumping enough ocean to wash away
a hundred thousand lives, most of them children,

and a million homes besides. The sea
returns in time the mercifully drowned:

those who remain are those who must endure
the loving care of God. If your daughter asked for
    bread

would you give her a stone? Then how much more
will be the anguish of the father

in the eyes of his dying child
for whom he can do nothing? If the poor

are so blessed, Andrew, thank God he does not often
    send
beatitudes as wonderful as this.

8

The siren voices of false certainty
re-phrase with seamless arguments

the serpent's many-layered lie
to each succeeding generation. Goebbels,

Saatchi and the hosts of cults and gurus
prove and reprove the prophet's words—

"a man hears what he wants to hear
and disregards the rest". The last

tragedy in Eden was not the fall
from innocence, but the deal itself:

the fruit was rotten. The knowledge
for which Adam sacrificed his all turned out to be

no more than gullibility—having swallowed the apple
it seems we'll swallow almost anything.

9

So much that at one time seems unassailable
flickers and fades like a dream. We were conceived

in the womb of relative ignorance, inheritors
of certain sets of workable hypotheses—

a shopping-trolley loaded with beliefs—
and in the trials of circumstance our faith

or its nonentity is shaped by what happens to us,
or driven by it flat into the ground. The

lightning flashes of experience
illuminate the chasm that divides

our creed from what we actually believe—
orthodoxy and atheism are alike,

tents where a refugee faith camps
out of the unrelenting weather of the harder questions.

10

You're writing about marriage—there's a double irony
I know you'll smile at! You, the one-time model
    bachelor! But then

that it should be the issue that broke
you from your first church—that's a tougher one.

Of course the dogma puts half America
into spiritual no-man's land—*Shouldn't*'s a poor sermon

for those who've vowed and failed, and try again;
in the bed they've made (if you'll forgive the metaphor)

they have to find some way to lie. Whatever you write,
    Andrew,
I hope there'll be comfort "for our hardness of heart".

There's no Eden to go back to. The apple
has been eaten, from its thrown core

those trees have grown on whose fruit we have to live,
our only *Sitz im Leben* is in their shade.

11

The world is spoiled and cannot be redeemed
piecemeal by liberal or green do-goodery. Graphs

grow exponentially, earth
performs its great strip-tease, and for a finale

will disappear up its own backside
with quite astonishing ease, to the applause

of constant economic growth. False Christs
queue at Burger King; the elect

wander in the myths of Sunday colour magazines
reading of earthquakes and rumours of wars

in which the disarmed ideologies embrace
beneath the icons of material prosperity—this
    abomination

that brings desolation, this god of matter
to whose altar we have been dragged smiling to be
    sacrificed.

12

What little I know of scientific method
tells me a theory is no use that only fits

ninety-five per cent of the results—
it's in the other five that truth lies, Andrew,

on the margins of experience
our gospel is defined. In the Gadarene tombs

Christ and the madman have finished their business
and while we, clothed and in our right minds

consider what it means for us here and now
he has given us the slip, crossing

the dark, storm-bothered waters of Gennesaret
to 42nd Street and Auschwitz: the pimps, drunks,
    addicts,

psychotics, murderers and those whom they destroy,
these will be redeemed, or nobody at all.

13

The ark sailed sometime in the 1980s.
The animals went in two by two

or seven by seven depending on which source takes
     precedence:
its motley cargo—Jonah's fish, Job's friends,

ten-foot Goliath, Balaam's talking ass,
limping Jacob, branded Cain, the subtil snake, even

the primal pair themselves, naked and unashamed—
all herded in with Noah and his sons.

That clear blue evangelical assurance
clouded over with the cumulus

of archaeology and reasoned common sense
in ever-darkening folds; beneath its weight

the heavens bowed. The muddy deluge broke. The ark
sailed out of history and into myth.

14

Here, Andrew, is the plain good news—God
died immortal, loves all men equally

and some more equally than others,
comes not to judge but to judge, brings peace

with a sword, frees us
into complete subjection where first

is last, poor rich, and folly wisdom, where at the end
all shall be united, and split up.

One God, three Gods, the riddle of the Trinity;
God-man, the paradox of incarnation;

King of a world ruled by somebody else,
who makes disciples of their own free will—this is

the God whom we believe and don't believe.
And this we call the simple gospel truth.

15

And still there is the old familiar puzzle:
how can he be omnipotent and good?

Did he use his power to manufacture evil?
Or have the will, but lack the means to stop it?

Or if, as it must be, neither can be true,
how should we comprehend this suffering God

who kills us with his endless loving-kindness? The
    question has
defeated the best minds that he made: this dreadful
    love

laid out the context for its own rejection, gave
to its beloved the gift of doubt, and mental tools

to fashion arguments to justify it; and then stood back,
watching as into the vacuum of its withdrawal

sin rushed like a wind, a kinetic power
as insubstantial as a hurricane.

16

One hundred million years ago
a diplodocus waded in the swamps

of Hammersmith, its tiny brain
untroubled by thoughts of God, who no doubt looked

as lovingly upon him as later
with tenderness he would watch over simple,

savage men at Easter Island or Stonehenge, their short
    lives
broken on the megaliths of their deeply held
    untruths—

for them it was not the *kairos*, the right time,
and no doubt they will be judged by their lights

in the folly of their generations
by this curious, demanding, secret God

who gazes down from somewhere as his universe
expands hopefully to meet him.

17

We must return to sources, to this holy
and wholly extraordinary book into which

we read back our favourite doctrines, sharing
the comfort of the party line, determined

to make life what we think it ought to be
until our faith becomes a form of words—this

is conspiracy, not truth: incarnation
does not come in a risk-free environment—

if God has delegated his authority
to a team of editors and correspondents

in different times and languages, is it
surprising that his trust should be repaid

with anomalies and factual mistakes? Even prophets
must be given freedom to be wrong.

18

It would be hard to get the New Testament convicted
on a charge of apostolic authority. Out of

nine or ten writers—not including *Q*—
four at most heard Jesus' promise

in the upper room, that "when the Spirit comes
he will guide you into all truth." The synoptics

all drew on unattributed pool reports, the Gentile Luke
took the whole thing down second-hand; Paul,

well we have his word for his apostleship—
in whatever sense you like—but who will vouch

for Mark? James? Jude? 2 Peter? Or could even guess
the writer to the Hebrews? I don't doubt

their inspiration, Andrew, but the doctrine's flawed;
no wise house could now be founded on such sand.

19

The Jews I think say there are
three meanings for anything in the Torah—

the plain sense, the prophetic
and the hidden, real significance—well, it's true

that Matthew's use of Scripture wouldn't last
five minutes in a sound Evangelical school!

In this debate at least, Andrew,
it's time that we put down this mongrel reason,

born out of Aristotle and Descartes,
cross-bred with Darwin, Freud and Jung—

slipping the leash of faith it has turned wild,
this pit-bull logic, with the jaws

of its *reductio ad absurdum* locked
on anything that might get in its way.

20

God had the choice of technologies. We could have
    received
the perfect, unambiguous written Word,

no missing Hebrew vowels or doubtful
readings, no variant manuscripts, disputed
    authorship—

the letters clearly signed by Paul or John
(or maybe Barnabas)—translated into

every language, with second copies placed
in safe deposit in case of accidents:

but this way he has given us his commandments
without tripping us up at the first—

or should we seek out some Aaron to re-cast
the golden idol of inerrancy,

and set it up and worship it amongst
the anachronistic stones of Jericho and Ai?

21

Who sanctions this search
for a systematic theology? Christ,

who talked in parables? Only God
could reconcile the strains of these

scholastic gymnastics, and knowing faith to be
more powerful than certainty

he chooses to do something else instead. Just as
his image persists within our sinfulness

so truth inhabits our ambiguous language,
truth that is not the whole truth,

and rarely nothing but the truth,
that in a fallen world can only be displayed

in an imperfect medium, and in its revelation
puts dogma on the rack, where it belongs.

22

Imagine one more myth. Suppose there was
an image, once, of perfect truth,

in which Adam looked, until like everything
it was shattered in the Fall, its pieces strewn

across the centuries. Most came to rest
in a small, untidy, squabbled-over country,

where men, by diligence or what seemed luck,
discovered fragments, stained or brightly polished,
      edges

sharp enough to wound; they swept-up sixty-six,
each one a book, and when with careful restoration

at Nicaea they had done the best they could
they held it up at last—the Bible, Paul's dark glass,

a broken mirror that somehow returns
the cracked reflection of the face of God.

23

We do not find God by theology
nor coax him out of hiding with our worship.

We discover him instead
in places that we least expect, where his power

is concealed by insignificance: in the little
act of kindness seeking no reward,

the momentary thought for others, obedience
in a thing thought trivial—matters

so small they are like
a medicine of such a weak solution

as to be hardly there at all, and traceable
by no known science—yet these are

our real investments, the widow's mites with which
he finances his kingdom's public spending.

24

That he should choose obscurity
comes as no surprise—the Jewish books

are testaments of the implausible,
their heroes a cast of rejects: Abraham

and his ancient, sterile wife;
the upstart Jacob; Moses, doubly an outcast;

Rahab the scheming prostitute; Gideon the feeble;
David the overlooked son; Ruth, widow, foreigner,

woman; and all the ragged conscripts of the prophets;
the divine script is the story of the blessed underdog—

even the chosen people themselves, a nation
of such global unimportance that successive conquerors

allowed them to continue in the worship
of their quaint, invisible and plainly harmless God.

25

The history of Israel is a black cloak of failure
patched with brief colours of brighter cloth—

covenants broken, the pointless
wandering in the desert,

anarchy under judges and the tragedy of kings:
Saul's madness, David's lechery,

Solomon and all his wives, and after them
the slow descent into apostasy,

dogs kept off by alliances with wolves.
Jerusalem defiled, ransacked, abandoned,

then painfully and partially restored—
if it seems familiar it is because it is

our own story, the tale of good intent
sacrificed to the idols of our selves.

26

From his first word
God's efforts to communicate hardly ceased.

His choice of media was comprehensive:
earthquakes, winds, floods, fires, still small voices,

burning bushes, tablets, parables,
plumblines, angels, donkeys, plagues and dreams,

potters' wheels, handwriting on the wall,
the quiet chat in the desert, the mass

meeting for the reading of the Law,
and then for five hundred years

pouring out through prophet after prophet
pleadings and promises and dire warnings

that bordered on despair—in all of this
the message never changed: return, be healed.

27

Finally it seemed God had given them up
and for four centuries there was no word,

just the crushing weight of military occupations,
like a dowry for this nation

that had married once too often
with foreign gods; in the Judaean hills

the Maccabeans chose out their Messiahs
and shook their swords at heaven for its silence.

But all this time God was gathering his breath
to speak his last tremendous word,

and when it was delivered
it was squeezed out from a single human body

in the only, painful way there is and laid out
helpless, derelict and in the heart of nowhere.

28

The word said "Become like this
or you will never find me—

if you are simple you will hear angels,
if you are wise you must watch for signs

and both will lead you to bring your questions
and lay them at this improbable manger

where I have placed the passion
that will consume all of mankind. This is what I mean

when I say the kingdom of heaven
is like a mustard seed, that it is

folly to the wise and a stone on which
the righteous will stumble, for I have not come

for the righteous, of whom there are none,
but to save sinners, of whom there are already enough."

29

The word was squeezed out like a drop
of ointment, a single spot

of water in the desert, or the first tiny crack
in the fault before an earthquake; the word was

a whisper barely audible, but in the hollow
of our hearts it echoed, and the echo grew

to a sound that made the whole world
stop its ears in case its ringing should crack

the deep glazing of our self-satisfaction and into
our earthen vessels pour its treasure. The word

broke in like a visitation of angels,
its bright light scattering the thin

flocks of our achievements that we graze
so carefully in high, unfriendly pastures.

30

"Fear not" the herald said—yet until then
I think the shepherds were quite unconcerned.

Cold, perhaps, or quarrelsome, or bored, but not
expecting anything to happen, and anxious

only for the usual domestic reasons. What scared them
was the sight of their clean, familiar sky ripped open

by beings from another dimension,
brilliant with the news that God

has become a man, and is quite unlike
anything that we expected—this is something

to be afraid of, Andrew, this rude
intrusion into the world we thought we had created:

the owner has turned burglar, breaking in
to steal our Chubb-locked hearts, and throw the keys
    away.

31

The ark sailed backwards through the centuries
beyond the reach of modern scholarship: Einstein

discovered nothing to which it was related, Galileo
failed to trace its course in the stars, da Vinci

could only speculate on its design, Columbus
was the boldest, with the least successful result—

and when it was found at last,
by the shepherds acting on a tip-off,

it was much smaller than we had imagined, just
a wooden box, with a few beasts attending,

hardly adequate, you'd think, for the deliverance
of all humanity from the flood of judgement,

its single occupant asleep, and over all the covenant
        sign,
not a rainbow but Golgotha, the soul's true Ararat.

32

This was no rehearsal. Failure was possible
but he could not fail—his strength

became his weakness, for he knew
the power of unlimited temptation

but not the luxury of giving in; he met
human kind in its squalor and brutality

and took exception only to its pride.
And our lives are no rehearsal: unlike

the Irishman giving directions we can't say
"I wouldn't start from here"—he

won't wait for us to become respectable
but finds us, like Zacchaeus, up a gum tree

or the woman in her well of promiscuity, places where
we can hardly bear his failure to be shocked.

33

The Bible says Jesus loved Lazarus so much
that, hearing he was ill, he stayed away

just long enough for him to die. The sisters'
grief turned to anger and confusion, knowing

that it need not have been so—Mary
fell at his feet with a sullen

ignorant rebuke: "Lord, if you had been here..."
And we are Mary. Her four days' despair

has been drawn out in us for two millennia,
the word we sent remains unanswered while

those that are loved go to their certain
deaths—he will come again

when it all seems much too late, shouting
"Come out" to a bound and stinking world.

34

These poems should have been about the cross,
    Andrew,
but who could do that? We, who wait here

in its long shadow, trying to look up
and unable, knowing that to gaze directly at it

will burn out the pupils of our self-esteem? It is not
finished: that face (R S Thomas said it) is "staring

as over twenty centuries it has stared,
from unfathomable darkness into unfathomable light",

while we between both look on, helpless
like children in Dickens, bewildered heirs

to some great estate, watching
the tragic tale unfold, knowing

our future joy depends on this transaction
in whose genesis we are somehow implicated.

35

Put down this bag of words,
coins for a potter's field. Whose

likeness do they bear? God is diminished
by all our explanations: we have made

Christ in our own image, scourged him
with the whips of our doctrines, wrapped

his beaten body in our purple prose,
frozen his agony in window glass

and made the cross a trinket. In all we know
there is no analogue for Calvary:

but for three hours on a Friday afternoon
Jerusalem lay in unearthly darkness

then on a scaffold the eternal word
hung silent, staring, gape-mouthed, perfectly dead.

36

We move with a certain grace, like skaters
going quickly on the thin ice

of our lives and theology, afraid
of what might happen if we stop too long

to contemplate the depths beneath. This
picture, drawn by a dying woman, pulls apart

the brittle surface of our lives to show
the gaps in our broken world let in no darkness

but the light that always shines
unseen behind it; its jagged

border frames the outline of a body
created purely out of pain; and that

the pieces of our lives are held in place
by what so often looks just like his absence.

37

This is where faith begins,
not during some religious palaver

when our thoughts are on their Sunday best behaviour,
but at a rubbish tip outside a city. Three figures

approach a fourth sitting alone, and the huge
silence of the ancient world is pierced

by Job's unintelligible howl of pain, the cry
of faithful ignorance, the unanswerable question

"Why have you forsaken me?" hanging in the air
for its answering echo, a thousand years later

from another rubbish tip outside another city. This is
the place of sacrifice to which we bring

our most-cherished theories, caught like Isaac's ram
in the impenetrable thicket of good and evil.

38

For what is it we pray? That peace
will come, and prophecy go unfulfilled?

For the unchangeable to change his mind?
In a game of blind man's buff

beneath the storms of God we hide
or lay out the tarpaulin of our prayers

and catch what grace we can, asking
"that it will not be in winter",

and though our intercessions seem as futile
as five small loaves among five thousand men,

he breaks the bread of our prayers
to feed the hungry who come

to eat, gathered so far out
at the edge of the soul's miraculous hillside.

39

I'm no raving charismatic (as you know!)
but what dogma brings you—David Watson's curate—

to say some gifts are not
for us here and today? What then

are these signs? Wishful thinking?
Something worse? Would you confine

his supernatural utterances to one time and place,
say that the God of Job is bound

to speak now only after proper exegesis? Andrew,
in God's supreme untidiness I only see

he will do what he wants to when he wants to,
and speak in whatever tongue or form of silence

best suits his purpose to confound
our stolid pharisaic study of divine behaviour.

40

Our African friend Kenneth says
his church depends on spiritual power

because they've no money for medicines.
Our sceptical analysis is nothing more

than the reasoning of the rich, who have placed
their faith in the NHS and BUPA

to insure against such acts of God.
These healings are

like early blossom of a coming summer:
this is his nursing love, to ease

the symptoms of a dying world, where health
is a mercy and not a right; and where although

the antidote was given long ago, it still appears
sin's virulence must run its bloody course.

41

For two thousand years
we seem to have got it wrong—the cherished

wisdom of one century becomes
anathema to the next. God

is someone immeasurably greater
than we might conceive, who does not need

all our apologetics and leaves us just
the truth that we can bear.

These brooding contradictions are our guides
through the doorway of salvation,

and somewhere out of time the whole
unjust distribution of resources

will be safely gathered up—Tessa once said
the plural of paradox must be paradise.

42

You won't take offence at this, I'm sure,
from one who "hides God's counsel without
    knowledge"!

Out of the mental whirlwind he still speaks
the words of eternal life—humble,

unanswerable. Heaven's wonders are not learned
in any college or debate, but in

our everyday endurance where we gain
the few things that are needful: faith

that will outstare the frozen gaze of logic; hope
that hangs on when sense is beaten; love

that fashions out of human anguish
the material of eternity—these three remain,

and Corrie ten Boom's words, "the closer you get to
    God
the less you understand, the more believe."

43

A friend gave me this picture,
that like Ezekiel's river from the temple

the clear torrent of the Spirit pours down
the stony channels of our enterprise

and all our arguments amount
to a few old rusty implements, blunt shears and rakes

stuck in the river bed, and of no more use
than knives to slice waves from a waterfall. Here

in the sunny silence of a winter afternoon
outside this upper room the trees stretch out

as if in supplication. These words are scattered
in the valley of dry bones, waiting

for the rustling of the wind of God, waiting
for the coming spring, the breath of Pentecost.

44

Eleven thirty. Tessa lies with eyes closed
fighting a fever, mine open at my book wrestling

with the Welsh priest-poet's images of God.
The little girl comes in, her pale face

serious: "I want a cuddle"—she wriggles
down into the gap between us. "Did you have

a bad dream?" "Yes." "What was it about?"
"I don't know." She lies there still, the warmth

of our closeness all the comforting she needs.
And I don't know what it was about,

the guilt, the bargaining, all that wasted time
spent second-guessing God: the Father loves us

as I love Emma and Joel—not because
they're good or clever, but because they're mine.

45

I remember how one night some years ago,
driving alone on the M25, I saw

a 747 blinking in the sky and thought of you
flying back from America, those dreams

broken like stubborn heresies, your seeming failure
broadcast to those who love you,

Katherine and Charlotte a consolation, with all
your fragile certainties intact and still

convinced of our gift for sin. The lights
of Heathrow beckoned someone home—it might

be you or me up there in all that darkness,
aching for landing, locked into that beam

as keen as radar, drawing us slowly down
in endless circles, moths to His great flame.

Welcome to the real world

As for man, his days are like grass,
he flourishes like a flower of the field;
the wind blows over it and it is gone,
and its place remembers it no more.
But from everlasting to everlasting
the Lord's love is with those who fear him.

Psalm 103, 15-17

These poems were written between 1992 and 2000.

Light of the World (1992), *Skin* (1995), *Baby crying* (1996), *The last straw* (1997) and the *Magi* sequence (1998) were written for carol services at St John's, West Ealing.

Welcome to the real world and *Creed* were written for the event *Welcome to the real world* at St Johns in 1993. *The Trinity monologue* was written for Trinity Sunday there in 1998.

Love reaches out is the title poem from a multimedia production with songs by Donald McRobbie, first produced at St Johns in 1998. *Communiqué* (also for this production) was written following the Good Friday agreement in Northern Ireland. A CD of the music from *Love reaches out* is available from Wordsout.

Song at the start of a century: This poem in two voices borrows the style of the New York poet Walt Whitman (1819-92). Unless explicitly attributed, the italicised words of the second voice are my own, except for the lines from the Lord's Prayer and the sequence beginning *The unthinkable becomes thinkable*, the source of which I do not know.

Glasnost (*Glasnost, 1993*), meaning openness, was a keyword of the Soviet regime prior to the collapse of communism in 1989.

Dear son was written for the dedication of my son Adam.

Adore your door, Reaching, Keys and *Only wood* were written for the poetry/mime production *Only Wood* (1995) with John and Carina Persson.

Bernhard Langer (*Bernhard Langer approaches Sarajevo*) won a major golf tournament at the time of the Bosnian war in 1993.

The title *Truce with the Furies* is derived from the title of R S Thomas' last collection, *No Truce with the Furies*.

The cure and *From where she lies* were written for my mother Joan.

Five candles was written for Graham and Karen Taylor-Burge and is published with their kind consent.

Act One

Bang!

God laughed
and millions of galaxies
spiralled away like firecrackers
into the curving dark.

How's *that!*
said God,
to nobody in particular.

God considered
nobody's point of view.
His best idea
simmered
in the slow cooker
of evolution.
Turning the dial
to *interactive*
he brought it to the boil.

Ah, men!
beamed God,
and settled himself down
with his freshly-made audience
to enjoy the show.

But the players hadn't learned their lines.
Creation began to unravel
before God's widening eyes,
spectators coolly hardening
into critics.

Out of Eden

The shores of Lake Victoria
are beautiful, but red.
The birth of human being
happened hereabouts, it's said.

Rwanda's latest harvest
is laid neatly out in rows—
blood's thicker than water,
as everyone now knows.

Someone fired the pistol
and no-one holds the ring—
the hounds of hell are playing,
the party's in full swing.

Neighbour turns to neighbour,
Abel turns to Cain.
It's the old familiar story
out of Eden once again—

it's the lesson unforgotten,
the elemental part:
prayers can move the spirit
but machetes touch the heart.

Welcome to the real world

I'm beginning to understand.
I saw a sign once
outside a church. It said
Are you really living
or just walking around
to save the expense of a funeral?

I didn't know
that Love is real life,
and everything else
just a more or less entertaining way
of dying.

And I didn't know
that Love is like nothing on earth.

Love isn't what you fall in.
It's what pulls you out
of what you fall in.

Love isn't a good feeling.
Love is doing good
when you're feeling bad.

Love means hanging in
when everyone else
shrugs their shoulders
and goes off to McDonalds.

Love means taking the knocks
and coming back
to try to make things better.

Love hurts.
It's its way of telling you
that you're alive.

And the funny thing is that after all
Love does feel good.
People say Love is weak.
But Love is tougher than hate.
Hating's easy.
Most of us have a gift for it.

But Love counts to ten
while Hate slams the door.
Love says *you*
where Hate says *me.*

Love is the strongest weapon
known to mankind.
Other weapons blow people up.
Only Love puts them back together again.

And everything that seems real,
that looks smart,
that feels good,
has a sell-by date.
But Love has no sell-by date.
Love is Long Life.
Love is the ultimate preservative.

I don't know too much about Love
but I know a man who does,
up there on the cross
loving us to death.

Love is the key
to the door of the place
he's prepared for you
in the kingdom of God.

If you're beginning to understand
then welcome to the real world.

Saved in Japan

"In the hotel room of the future
Gideon's Bible will have a rival—
Nintendo video games" (News item)

The marketplace was crowded
and the competition real,
so the Gideons and Nintendo
sat down and made a deal.

It seemed a smart alliance
of such very different aims—
a God-and-mammon enterprise:
Nintendo Bible games!

Gameboy David v Goliath,
Moses' Race Across The Sea,
Donkey-Kong's-Search-For-A-Stable,
Armageddon-Home-For-Tea.

Now the weary business traveller
seeking spiritual dole
could find fun *and* consolation
in a hand-held game console.

The reviews were all terrific,
salesmen's expectations high—
yet the project was a failure
and nobody quite knew why.

All of Webworld's smartest hackers
couldn't tell how it was done—
but no matter who was playing
somehow Israel *always* won.

Absalom

Fall, flood, Babel;

and Abraham begat Ishmael
and Isaac begat Esau
and Jacob begat Judah

and David begat Absalom,
the virus more resistant

                     in each generation.

O Absalom,
my son, my son

the cosmic shambles,
the unpronounceable

                  invisible YHWH,
ever faithful

        destroyer of nations.

O my children
be blessed
be blessed

or else

Love reaches out

What was God doing
as he studied the victims
of the latest Extreme
Weather Event?

What was God doing
for the carefree child
running into the road
just as the car accelerated?

What was God doing
while the fittest worked out
their next brutal plan
of survival?

These questions will not be answered today
or any other day.
But something happens
when love reaches out.

A hand stretches down
from the rescue craft.
Tears sting
behind the eyes.

Something breaks
when love reaches out.
It might be a heart,
or a burst dam of pride.

Love overthrows
the government of fear.
If your hands are full
what can you reach for?

Your trophies and pride
will be scattered about
when you reach out for love,
or when love reaches out.

Light of the World

Let there be light, he said.
Ah, but what sort of light?
That's where we come in.
Allow me to introduce myself:
Senior Consultant,
Cherubim & Seraphim Technical Services.
Sound and lighting engineers by appointment to the
     Almighty.
Special rates for miracles and plagues.
Discount on all feedings of five thousand or more
and free thunderbolt with each repeat order.

No doubt you're familiar with our past productions.
We did the whole screenplay for the Tower of Babel.
With subtitles, of course.
The story of Noah.
Floodlit.
And Sodom and Gomorrah—
one of our most successful features.
An epic of biblical proportions according to the critics.
Not that there were many critics left afterwards.
And of course the Wilderness Wanderings.
Low budget series, but it ran and ran.
Forty years lit by a single pillar of fire
and a seven-branched candelabra.

But that was all before privatisation.
Lighting's a tough business these days.
Lots of competition.
It's a jungle out there in the desert.
So many options, you see—
sunlight, moonlight,

street light, neon light,
Budweiser Light.
You've got to be in there
with this new-fangled electricity.
Anyway, that's the current thinking.

Now this new script—
strangest of the lot.
The Nativity.
Don't know where he gets these ideas from.

Scene 1. Shepherds watching.
Gabriel, with backing vocals.
Need a good clear sky for that.
No interference from satellite tv.
Quick burst of heavenly host, then blackout.
Music from the Hallelujah Chorus?
No, Handel hasn't been born yet,
it'll have to be something by Cliff.
It was much simpler in Moses' day.
No 747s over Cairo airport—
anything flying at night had to be an angel.

Scene 2. Wise men searching.
(Shouldn't that be *Why are men searching?*).
Ought to have direct sunshine,
but humans can't look straight the sun.
Have be the light of faith then.
Soft starlight should be enough,
with a single, moving follow-spot.

Scene 3. King Herod's Palace.
Well, someone's taken his grumpy pills this morning!
Torches will do for him.
Lots of flickering flames—
Herod needs to get used to working in a hot place.
Then cue the dream sequence
and Magi leave by a side exit.

Scene 4. A packed public house.
No problem getting atmosphere for this:
Jukebox playing *Little Donkey*.
TV in the corner showing rerun of David v Goliath
    championship fight.
Enter distressed couple, woman heavily pregnant.
Unable to get near bar.
Clearly they don't drink Carling Black Label.
Artificial lights for this one.
People don't want to see too clearly
when they're enjoying themselves.
Big glowing EXIT sign:
This way for a stable relationship.

Final Scene. The Nativity.
Total darkness?
Well there's a challenge.
This must be his avant-garde period.
I should be grateful at least he's not filling the stage
with children and animals.
Oh.
Why does he do this, just when it needs
a big number to wind things up?

Not exactly prime time material:
a finale with one 40-watt bulb
resting on a sleeping ass.
He'll be crucified in the ratings.
Never mind.
I've put in for the contract to light the Book of
     Revelation.
That's bound to be a showstopper.

Hold on.
Here's one more stage direction.
Enter the Light of the World.

Ah.
That should be quite effective.
Yes, that ought to do the trick.

I wonder if St Michael has any vacancies in
     merchandising?

Baby crying

The scene is familiar. A baby is sleeping.
His mother's worn out. It's been a hard day.
A few hours before she was groaning and weeping,
just a child, giving birth in the usual way.

The place doesn't matter, except it's not cosy
the way that the prettiest Christmas cards say,
with kings humbly kneeling, the stable all rosy,
the little Lord Jesus asleep on the hay.

Forget the carol constructed so neatly—
the cattle are lowing, the baby awakes.
Forget the Sundayschool singing so sweetly
that *little Lord Jesus no crying he makes.*

The baby is crying. The baby is human
and the baby is God and he cries with the shock.
He cries for the keys to his coming kingdom.
He cries for the devil who first picked the lock.

He cries for the mother whose heart will be broken.
He cries for the children whom Herod will find.
He cries for the father whose fears are unspoken
but for ever will prey on his uncertain mind.

He cries for food in a land ploughed by famine.
He cries for freedom behind a barred door.
He cries for a judge who will come and examine
the reasons for sin and the causes of war.

He cries for the rich who on hearing him crying
lean over and say *There now, give us a smile!*
He cries for the camps full of refugees dying—
his tears are the Congo, the Danube, the Nile.

He cries for us, pharisees, each of us giving
the reasons why sadly we have to refuse.
He cries out for Lazarus, both dead and living.
He cries for two thousand years of excuse

and our patience is thin as a sliver of glass
as we fear this child's crying will never die down.
It slithers through time as a snake slips through grass:
he would cry us an ocean in which we would drown

except it subsides. The baby is quiet.
Stillness returns to the primitive night.
Whatever is coming he will not defy it
for he came after all to put everything right.

He cries for the strength that he needs to prepare him
to learn obedience in thirty long years.
Good Friday will come. Death will not spare him.
The world will at last be baptised with his tears.

His crying at night is his effort to waken
the sleeping and dead whom he came to live through.
He cries to the God who must leave him forsaken.
He cries out to me. He cries out to you.

Bring on the dancing vicar

Bring on the dancing vicar,
keep them rolling in the aisle!
The time goes by much quicker
in the service with a smile.

Call up the chuckling curate—
let humour be ordained!
We really can't endure it
unless we're entertained.

Lead in the laughing pastor
with the twinkle in his eye!
Get those punchlines coming faster,
make us howl until we cry.

Keep the congregation keener
I say! I say! I say!
Skip the bread and the Ribena,
let's just have the cabaret.

Crabs

The reason crabs
are so crabby
is that they're just
completely
shellfish

Come on in, the sofa's lovely

When the belt around your belly sidles out another
    notch
and the footballers on telly are the sons of those you
    watched,
when your clothes are back in fashion and you never
    even knew
and the high point of your Saturday's a trip to B&Q,

when the grown-ups at your parties are outnumbered
    by their kids
and you notice that prime ministers look younger than
    they did,
when you catch yourself complaining that a programme
    goes too far
and insist a Ford Mondeo's really quite a stylish car,

when a hit song sounds like someone with a terminal
    disease
and you find that you're agreeing with Conservative
    MPs,
when a singer makes a comeback and you didn't know
    he'd gone
and your daughter's latest boyfriend's never heard of
    Elton John,

when your favourite tv series only shows on UK Gold
and those other people at your school reunion look so
    old,
when you're free to stay up partying all night, but
    somehow don't
and your children are all big enough to wear your
    clothes, but won't,

when there's no-one to complain about the company
    you keep
and the most seductive reason for an early night is
    sleep,
when you'd write your masterpiece if you'd the leisure
    to begin it
and you'd have a mid-life crisis if you only had a
    minute

and you wonder what became of all that time that lay
    ahead
and all the things you could have done (and all the
    things you did instead),
then the hour has come at last to face the unforgiving
    truth
that your membership's expired of that exclusive club
    of *youth*.

Don't shake your balding head or stamp your Hush
    Puppies in rage—
look on it as *maturing* past that awkward, childish
    stage—
in the stuffing of life's turkey, just accept that you're
    the sage—
face the camera, smile and say that you're *approaching*
    middle age…

An exponent of the Prosperity
Gospel replies to the Beatitudes

Paul's First Fax to the Thessalonians

Another show was over,
the twenty-seventh on the Galilean tour.
Peter and James were loading the gear.

"Do we always have to use your Dad's van?"
Nathaniel asked Andrew.
"It stinks of fish."

"These outdoor gigs are getting me down"
said John.
"Five thousand people and no crèche facilities."

"We need something in the contract about the catering"
muttered James,
dumping another basket of leftover bread rolls.
"And a bigger PA system".

"I'm doubtful"
said Thomas.

"It'd be tax deductable"
said Matthew.

"Well I'm not too keen"
said Simon (the Zealot).

"It's no problem,
I can fix a loan"
said Judas,
reaching for his mobile phone.

Song at the start of a century
(Have a nice day, Walt Whitman)

Now that the calendar has granted us an opportunity
    for celebration,
which is several years late according to the best
    estimates,
and carries all the significance of a car's milometer
    clicking over to a particular string of zeroes,
let us embrace the accident of convenient numbers and
    sing at the start of a century!

My song has a target audience.
It is not for the family which smilingly eats the latest
    breakfast cereal together,
and for whom the choice of a new brand of dishwasher
    powder is a significant and life-enhancing decision,
for I say unto you, they have their reward.

> *Just when you thought no soap powder could wash any*
> *   whiter,*
> *when your woollens have so much bounce you have to*
> *   strap them down in the chest of drawers,*
> *around the lid of your shaving foam it says Good*
> *   Morning to you in four different languages—*

And it is not for the young man driving a fast car with
    an open roof,
whose companion's long hair will later be rinsed clean
    of atmospheric pollution by a widely-advertised
    type of conditioning shampoo,
for I say unto you, they have their reward.

Just when your dog's favourite food is the first choice
    of eleven out of ten breeders,
when you thought no biscuit could give you another
    crumb of comfort,
then we bring you one more flavour to savour,
turning towards the camera, our smiles, like our
    snacks, now even cheesier—

It is for the small and ordinary and bewildered.
It is the voice of one crying in a maisonette:

Where are you, Katie of the Oxo ads,
shaking your head indulgently at Philip,
whose pains could all be cured by Anadin?
Our souls cry out for you!

The blueprint of the last century was drawn in the one
    before—
Darwin selected it from disconnected bones,
Babbage computed its parameters,
Daguerre snapped its image on his photographic plate,
Bell rang it up demanding *Come here I need you,*
Freud placed it on his couch and checked its bank
    balance.
As an infant, Wilbur and Orville flew it in the rain at
    Kitty Hawk—

So many of the children died young.
Only the lucky survive—little Josef, little Adolf, little
    Vladimir Ilyich.
Benito is a darling, but so bossy!
He'll be a leader one day, you'll see!

The century was shaped by those who dreamed of a
    new order
and by those who saw that such a thing must be
    opposed,
who guessed that a change of heart was easier in a
    medical than a spiritual operation,
that we could split matter in two leaving the mess all
    over the Pacific,
and that finally we would sit at our private screens,
staring at our most intimate reflections, secure at last in
    the anonymity of total revelation.

> *We worship daily at the shrine of our one-eyed*
> *   household god.*
> *We pray by phone or postcard, though seldom get an*
> *   answer.*
> *The chosen ones win holidays or seats at football*
> *   matches.*
> *It is encouraging how readily our children have taken*
> *   to this religion.*

Of course we ration what the children watch—
no sex or violence or mindless rubbish
only positive stuff like nature programmes,
where animals mate and kill and eat each other up.

> *Have your credit card ready and call toll free!*
> *Now back to New York and here's Matt!*
> *Missing you already!*

And all new knowledge breaks existing laws,
and later everyone will say they knew it all the time.

Confucius he say
the superior man understands what is right,
the inferior man understands what will sell.

The Iron Curtain has been torn down and replaced
   with one bought from Ikea,
where at least former communists will find the length
   of queues reassuring,
and everyone is famous now for less than fifteen
   minutes.

   Phil Spector he say
   Da doo ron ron ron,
   da doo ron ron.

The European Community has been lost in translation,
standing in line at Brussels airport as taxis stream past
   the hoardings of its endless construction.
A Dane remonstrates with a Spanish colleague about
   the actions of the Nomination Committee
while the cold wind jumps the long queue and combs
   out his thinning hair.

   Joni Mitchell she say
   it's just a borderline,
   another borderline.

America eats a glazed donut in Penn Station,
waits for a taxi outside Madison Square Gardens,
is taken by a turbanned driver across Brooklyn Bridge,
beneath which Walt Whitman's ghost rides the ferry, his
   crocodile eyes twinkling.

> *In the land of the free, community is defined by*
> *   byelaws;*
> *we take an interest in you only if you do not have the*
> *   necessary paperwork,*
> *or if you will help us stop people doing something,*
> *otherwise in every possible respect you are on your*
> *   own ☺.*

And every screw-up is a commercial opportunity,
and every bankruptcy an incentive.
The great high priest of the market will give you
    absolution,
and every bagel vendor will have his IPO.

> *All you need is money.*
> *All you need is money.*
> *All you need is money.*
> *All you need is money.*

The average income of the world's poorest fifty
    countries is a dollar a day;
entire nations inhabit the tiny margins of currency
    fluctuations,
breathing in shallow fractions of a euro, dollar or yen.

> *Forgive us our debts,*
> *as we forgive those*
> *who forgive our debts.*

No-one is minding the store.
Not those who sit in panelled board-rooms, or give
    instructions to their overworked assistants.

The brightest minds are forming global strategies for
    marketing stupid but winsome cuddly toys.
The economies of whole continents survive on the
    things that destroy them,
tobacco, alcohol, cocaine and tourists hoovering up
    culture;
this is progress and the world into which we joyfully
    bring our slippery and wrinkled newborn babies,
and do so at a rate which is mathematically
    unsupportable.

    Remember, one thousand million Chinese can be
        terribly wrong.

In 99 years a hundred metres will be run in eight
    seconds by a woman.
In 99 years a computer the size of a matchbox will
    manage Europe.
In 99 years we will take our holidays on the Norwegian
    Riviera while our holograms keep our
    appointments at virtual business meetings.
In 99 years we will choose the colours of our children's
    eyes and be afraid to look into them.

    The unthinkable becomes thinkable.
    The thinkable becomes see-able.
    The see-able becomes do-able.
    The do-able becomes done.
    The done becomes the done thing.

The West's strategy is to pull the covers over its head
    and call for momma,

and momma comes bringing baseball caps and a
      hundred kinds of beer.
Entertainment is anaesthetic so we feel no pain
but run on like an athlete with cortisone injected into
      each of his rupturing joints.

> *Church Father Julian he say*
> *The world is at its last gasp*
> *(though to be fair he said this 16 centuries ago).*

Those who control people become almost
      undetectable.
Networks mate and reproduce and the air chokes with
      data.

> *Paul Simon he say*
> *These are the days of miracles and wonder*
> *and don't cry, baby, don't cry.*

The baby lives because of a medical breakthrough
for the lack of the price of which in another country a
      hundred children daily drink a deadly water
      cocktail,
and the transplant patient's doctor calls with good
      news:
someone has died, young and healthy in a road
      accident!

> *History in the real world is the history of women*
> *bearing sorrow.*
> *It is passed down in the pain of childbirth from*
> *mothers' mothers' mothers.*

The child's body nurtured for two decades then let go,
to be exploded in a moment or sent home broken
beyond repair.

That was the first century that has been reviewed in
real time,
and this will be the first to be replayed in real time.
We rebuild the images of our virtual past until it we
cannot tell it from the actual,
and everything will be connected to everything else
from an infinite number of points of view.

The Julian of Norwich chat room say
All shall be cool,
And all manner of thing shall be cool.

We have unlocked the secrets of the births of suns,
and plumbed the immensity of space,
but is it greater than the distances travelled across the
cold expanse between the still-forming stars of the
mind's nebulae?
In these days of limitless technology the artist still
sketches the bird,
and the camera films the artist sketching,
and we look through the camera at the artist sketching
the bird
and we sense the disproportion but do not laugh.

Rihaku he say
what is the use of talking,
there is no end of talking
there is no end of things in the heart.

And a place is just a co-ordinate on a map until it is
     understood with sorrow:
Aberfan Belsen Chernobyl Dunblane Enniskillen
     Galipoli Hiroshima Jonestown Kosovo Lockerbie
     MyLai Nagasaki Omagh Passchendaele Stalingrad
     Vukovar Waco—
the alphabet is almost complete.

    Christ the universal son looks on from the scaffold of
       his terrible creation,
    while the women bear the pain of the God who dies of
       these injustices,
    and ambition rattles like dice at the foot of the cross.

And time is the greatest trick of all.
We think that to name it is to know it and that to
     measure it is to master it, and we are deceived.
It is the unwelcome companion that wakes us each
     morning to try out its latest product,
and remains at our heels until we lie down each night
     exhausted by its constant opportunities.
We mark its passing with rockets that flare and glitter
     amazingly and then are utterly gone.

    Michael Leunig he say
    Nothing can be loved at speed.

The train from Washington DC runs through places
     with long names and short histories,
past the trees in Maryland in late October
with leaves of every possible shade of yellow, gold, red,
     orange and vermilion,

which were there the day the motorcade passed by the
    grassy knoll,
and on the day when the smoke cleared at Gettysburg,
and on the day *Santa Maria* slipped out of the harbour
    at Cadiz
on a damn fool's errand searching for a damn fool's
    dream of gold.

    Bono he say
    Love is a comprehensive technology.

A gust of wind brings a storm of leaves onto the garden
and the trees in the park are stripped beneath an ice-
    blue sky.
We know the seasons of our life behave no differently,
    though we clutch at immortality:
our spring comes in our children, theirs in theirs.

    Deliver us from evil.

And the distance between two people is the space where
    love flourishes or dies according to what fills it,
and the price of love is unbearable,
and the world you have shown us is an illusion but it is
    all that we have,

    for thine is the kingdom,
    the power and the glory,
    for ever and ever.
    Amen.

Glasnost, 1993

Katerina (dark and pretty,
fiery-eyed and twenty-something)
used to be a dancing teacher
under state control.

Now she's free to make her choices,
circulates with business contacts
and in basques of shiny satin
bares more than her soul.

With a dancer's graceful moves she
takes off every item till with
legs spread for inspection all her
assets can be seen,

but in her thoughts (her one remaining
private place) reflects that this is
not exactly what she hoped that
openness would mean.

Brief encounter

He loved her
in silk and see-through lace,

he loved her
in suspenders and black stockings,

but most of all
he loved her
in inverted commas.

Creed

I believe
in Super Mario.

He changed my life that day
when I asked him to bounce into the heart
of my tv game console,
and things have never been the same.

Mario is my shepherd.
I shall not want
to go to bed.
He makes to stay up till four in the morning
trying to get to Level Three.
He leads me in the paths of sleeplessness
for his game's sake.

Mario dies for *my* mistakes!
Mario dies for me
but always rises again.
Resurrections are no big deal.
Mario's done them zillions of times.

Some people don't believe in Mario.
Some say he's just a crutch.
Some say he's a waste of time.
Some even say he doesn't exist.

But I know
that Mario can triumph over all evil,
so I give him the absolute devotion
of a true disciple.

I believe that one day I will play
the perfect game of Super Mario
and burst through to the final level
where Mario will go on for ever.

No longer will I gaze on Mario
as in a computer screen, darkly,
but then face to face.

I shall inherit eternal life
and will sit with my headphones and goggles on
at Mario's right hand
when he comes into his kingdom.

I want to live in Marioland for ever.
You're welcome to the real world.

Nursery haiku

Mums form a communion line—
the sacraments
Brio and coloured water.

Amongst the coats and boots
a smile of wonder
tucked in a bright red hood.

Walking home, lips sealed tight—
the marker pen
gives only name and number,

a private universe, clutching
bag and bunny,
hot hand gripping mine.

Dear son

Before you're old enough to answer back, I thought I'd better get in the advice a parent is supposed to give.

By the time you're five years old you'll know your dad is always right.

At eight you'll know your dad's usually right.

At twelve you'll know your dad is sometimes right.

At sixteen you'll know, with devastating certainty, your dad was never right about a single thing in his entire life. In fact you'll be convinced there was a mix-up at the hospital. You couldn't be genetically linked to anyone with such appalling dress sense and disastrous taste in music.

But that's all right. By twenty-five you'll realise he wasn't quite as hopeless as you'd thought, and by the time you pack him off to the Sunnydays Home for the Chronologically Gifted you'll almost have grown fond of the old fool.

So before this tiny window of opportunity slams shut on my fingers, here's something you ought to know.

Parenting's not easy. Even the word sounds like it's on probation from a social worker's handbook.

It was much simpler once. Dads went out to work, while mums stayed home and looked after the kids. There was a canny granny who knew a thing or two about colic and could wield a nappy pin without malicious damage.

Now mum's fulfilled by holding down a job, and
dad's a new man rushing home to change the babygros,
and both collapse at half past nine each night, racked
with guilt and haunted by the ghosts of their
inadequacy because Mum isn't running a small but
profitable chain of underwear boutiques, and Dad's not
Richard Branson (and frankly looks awful in those
chunky sweaters).

Help, though, is at hand. For godparents we have
Mothercare and the Early Learning Centre, and lots of
good advice from educationalists, psychologists,
anthropologists and out-of-work sociologists.

All of whom suggest we don't interfere.

Well, I'm going to. But the advice I'd like to give is
not the things at seventeen I swore I'd never say to my
kids. *Like Stop making all that noise*, or *Don't speak until
you're spoken to!*

(When you're older you might reflect on what
would happen if everyone obeyed that last instruction.)

That sort of advice is for the benefit of grown-ups
who'd like to judge you by appearances, and want you
to stay securely in your cot where they can keep a
watchful eye on you.

But I'm going to be your role model. Tough, I know,
but we'll have to make the best of it. I'll try to show
you some useful things that I've been shown myself.

Like what's right and wrong, and how to inherit eternal life. Just some stuff that wouldn't quite fit in the National Curriculum.

It isn't what you do that counts, but how you do it. So if you really want to dye your eyebrows turquoise, or set your heart on crossing the Gobi Desert on a camel, or even become an accountant, that's ok.

It isn't who you are that gets you anywhere, but who you follow. So don't be too concerned if, when your childhood's done, your end-of-term report says your achievements are quite limited.

You think two and two can make five.

You suppose the kingdom of heaven has a place in geography.

You mistake history for literature because *In the beginning was the word.*

You believe relativity has something to do with keeping a sense of proportion.

And in philosophy you hold the eccentric view that questions may somewhere have answers.

All in all you will be quite ill-adjusted to the expectations of society. And if that's the verdict then, dear son, I think that both of us will say we've come through pretty well.

The last straw
A narrative to introduce Christmas readings

The fall

From the very beginning
nothing was ruled out
and nothing ruled in
except choice;
but every choice
rules out another.

And so we are excluded
from the garden.
Peace is excluded.
Pain is included.
Time and death now are included.
Only love and its sacrifice
remains a choice
without limitation.

Genesis 3 1-15

Unto us a child is born

The damage spreads quickly.
As the sun of his presence
slips away, dark fingers
spread their dismal grasp
into every corner of our lives.

Still we call to one another
like children, lost upon a midnight moor,
piping up at any distant glimmer
that might be lights, or torches,
expecting at last
the footsteps of our father,
come to find and bring us home.

Isaiah 9 2,6-7

The word

Sometimes
words are not enough
for everything we have to say.

Words can't beat like a heart
A verb won't sweat or bleed.
A noun doesn't get thirsty.
An adjective cannot feel pain.
Something gets lost
in translation into words.

So when God
needed to express
a love deeper than words
he used body language
of a kind not known on earth before.

John 1 1-14

The Annunciation

Angels move
like electricity
and do not wear watches.

They are in the communications business.
They attend training courses
in calming startled humans.

They visit often
but are usually well disguised.
They have their work to do,

but now and then
they let the mask slip
to show their true identities.
They do this when it matters
that there should be no misunderstanding.

Some have seen angels.
Be humble and expect them
and they will come
in their own good time
or rather in God's time.

Luke 1 26-38

The Nativity

Was it necessary
to go to this extreme?
To take for a carrier
a village girl
unmarried and disgraced,
nine months pregnant
on an exhausting journey
to a strange town
with nowhere to stay,
in a century
with no healthcare
or sanitation?

What purpose was achieved,
except to show
how the weight of his love
is so exhausting
it will break the back
of our most stubborn pretensions
and how in a manger
would be the last straw to do it?

Luke 2 1-7

The shepherds

It was done plainly enough.
The night sky was a perfect billboard,
the sound effects spectacular.

Only a few were awake
and in the right place
at the right time when heaven,
unable to contain its amazement any longer,
spilled out momentarily into earth
and explained itself.

The message was clear as day
but his timing was, as always, surprising,
and the show ran
for one performance only.

Luke 2 8-20

The Magi

Will you study these signs
as carefully.
as you study the prices
in the Christmas catalogues?

Will you seek out the manger
as diligently
as you search for the right scarf
or this year's toy?

Will you examine
your heart's pilgrimage
and be sure towards what stable
it carries its precious gifts?

Will you be a wise fool
to seek out and follow
the strange star of truth
in a sky full of glittering lies?

Matthew 2 2-12

The flight to Egypt

A fairytale would end here
but this is not a fairytale.

The hunt begins
for this intruder
who has disturbed the balance
of heaven and earth.

Herod is only the first
to make him a refugee,
the infant boys of Bethlehem
only the first blood spilled
in the bloody pilgrimage
of heaven's exile
living rough and dying rough
from the borrowed stable
to the borrowed tomb.

Matthew 2 13-18

Adore your door

Hey there.
Isn't there someone
you've been taking for granted?
Isn't it time
you thought a little more
about your door?
In a recent poll
the door was voted
third most under-rated
piece of household furniture.
So here
at the *Friends of the Door*
we've brought you
fifty things for you to do
to make more of your door:
Open it.
Close it.
Open it again.
Walk throught it.
Talk to it.
Ring (twice if you're the postman).
Leave it on the latch.
Go back to check its locked.
Slam it.
Jam it.
Handle it
with care.
Hold your breath
and listen for a noise behind it.
Don't harm it.
Alarm it.
Unlock it and take it with you

to McDonalds.
Employ a local youth to stuff newspapers though a hole
    in it
taking care to tear the most interesting pages.
Look at it through a keyhole.
Lock it.
Don't knock it.
Make an entrance through it.
Slink out of it.
Ring it up
and see if it's home.
Rap it.
Catflap it.
Post a letter to it through it.
Hide two Jehovah's Witnesses behind it
then disconnect the bell.
Bang it.
Hang it.
Put your name on it
to make it feel like it belongs.
Catch it.
Latch it.
Stick a number on it
to let it know it counts.
Sand it.
Understand it.
Paint it red.
Paint it black.
Then take it to a Rolling Stones concert
to make it feel at home.
Scrub it.
Chubb it.

Maybe take it off its hinge
for a binge.
Don't fail it,
Yale it.
Nail 95 theses to it and start a new religion.
Hold it open for a friend.
Shut it on a salesman's foot.
Let it beat you at draughts.
Early in the morning
close it softly
so as not to wake it,
and last thing at night
don't forget to lock it
so no-one can break in
and put it in their pocket.
Don't ignore your door
but adore your door
if you only would—
it's only wood.

Reaching

Many times I have reached out my hand
only to draw it back unclasped

Many times I thought I had been understood
Many times I have been beaten back by the brutality of
        words

So many times I have reached towards the handle of
        the door

I have always expected something tremendous to
        happen
I have always thought I was preparing to make my
        entrance to where
behind the door
the wise and beautiful laughed together happily
and planned the secret order of the world

I have always thought when I opened the door
everything would change

Sometimes I wonder what prevents me
Is it what I remember?

I remember a child lying by its dead mother
I remember a momentary loss of concentration
I remember steel probing a soft spot on the skin
I remember the slight variation in tone of voice that
        marks the end of affection
I remember the strength of youth
I remember things that never happened

As a child I lay staring at the shadows of branches
thrown by the streetlamp onto the bedroom door,
behind which I knew someone was listening,
and I lay hearing my heartbeat,
watching the handle, waiting for it to turn

I remember remembering

Sometimes I remember to forget
and then I reach towards the handle of the door

So many times I have reached towards the handle of
        the door
that I have come to think the door is only something I
        remember
and if the handle had turned I would have been afraid

Many times I have hoped there was nothing behind the
        door
Even more than I want to change I do not want to
        change
and beyond the door may be nothing to reach towards
but only remembering

So many times I have reached towards the handle of
        the door
knowing as I reached I would not turn it
and yet I reached

And will go on reaching towards the handle of the door
for there is hope not in the door but in the reaching

Keys

The poor man has a single key
to his sad and wretched room.
The official man has a bunch of keys
and he rattles them like doom.
The family man has a ring of keys
to fence his life about,
but I need no key—
no lock can keep me out.

Chance is my counsellor,
Luxury my house,
Pleasure is my mistress,
Jealousy my spouse,
Pride is my sustenance,
Anger my advice,
Nothing my religion,
Everything my price.

Roll up, roll up—
everybody wins!
Faites vos jeux, mesdames messieurs,
Roll away your sins.
Everybody gets a prize
who plays my little game—
behind each painted door
the prize is just the same.

Pleasure

On Sunday afternoon
if I am in a grump
I give myself a treat
and go off to the dump.

I pack up all the papers.
I pull on my old slacks.
I put the garden debris
into big black plastic sacks.

Sort the cardboard boxes,
spill a drop of wine,
lots of glass and bottles—
surely not all mine?

With a sheet protecting
the floor from nasty gunk
I load the jolly Volvo
with a Volvo-load of junk.

The cheery council worker
waves me on my way—
if I only had more rubbish
I could go there every day!

Then on Tuesday after breakfast
I find a sheaf of fun
in stationery bliss
in W H Smith & Son.

I love the coloured refills,
the plastic folios,
the little packs of labels
set neatly out in rows,

and when the aisle is empty
I make a furtive raid
on the special top-shelf section
where ring-binders are displayed.

Sometimes I make a purchase,
more often I just browse,
for sadly there's a limit
to the filing I can house.

If I buy a new desk-tidy
or some Lever Arches, say,
then it only means more old stuff
that I'll have to throw away

so on Sunday afternoon
if I am in a grump
I give myself a treat
and go off to the dump…

Maps

To know the world without maps
with each place relative to every other

is God's privilege. Maps are a frame of mind.
To stretch earth's skin

on the rack of an appropriate projection,
pinned down by latitude and longitude

is false security. Courage goes
beyond the consolation of the atlas—

it was absence of maps
tormented those wise men, searching between

fear's cancer and a capricorn desire,
and drawn towards Bethlehem,

the real world's compass locked upon
its passionate, magnetic north.

Magi
Four poems for Christmas

You ask from whence we came—
from many places. Some are legends now,
some unremembered. You make us into kings.
We were not kings, not even of ourselves.
Were we from the east? That is a point of view.
We set out from where we were. You give us names
like Melchior and Balthazar,
but those were not our names. From time to time
we have been called by many names—
Plato, Confucius, Archimedes,
Copernicus, Galileo, Newton,
Descartes, Darwin, Einstein, Heisenberg.
How long did the journey take? Months? Centuries?
When does a myth take hold,
in a moment or a thousand years?
Though calendars and clocks may shepherd it
with careful numbers, yet in the wilderness
time howls like a pack of wolves. We heard it all night long.
We were both men and women. What we shared
was an unquenchable desire to know
something not known before. Were we wise?
Wise to leave our homes, acquaintances and all
the comfort of familiar irritations,
shedding the fabric of our former lives
like an old coat? To risk everything
on our unlikely theories
with no guarantee of safe return,
and reckless that the truth that we discover
may prove, for all we know, fatal
to everything to which we have thus far clung?
If this is wisdom, yes,
you may say that we were wise.

The journey

There were signs in the sky
but we misread them badly. For a long time we thought
the sun moved round the earth, and yet
our calculations showed up something wrong.
Like curious boys we took it all apart
piece by cosmic piece. Patiently we watched the stars,
carefully recording each small change
until the evidence was inescapable.
We dug up rocks and bits of bone,
but this made matters worse.
We broke them down into their elements
to see what they were made of—
earth, water, fire and air
did not stand up to cross-examination.
Anxious for tools we dreamed technology:
the microscope and telescope were two ways
of asking the same question. We carried on
through molecules, atoms and electrons
to quarks and antiquarks, the smallest stuff
that anyone could find, following
our star at speeds approaching light
between the particle and wave, where matter turns
to energy, and energy is all that matters.
It was much simpler when we could all believe
that stars were lamps and God the kindly lamplighter.
There had been wars, each one bloodier
than the last, but none as terrible
as standing on those borderlines of truth
and finding every one a cheap stockade
of prejudice and fear. We were burned
as heretics and witches, tortured,
excommunicated, ridiculed or quietly ignored.

When all humanity begged us to stop
we pressed on, into the human gene
and to the mapping of the mind.
We will uncover everything in our search
for something we can worship.
We have trampled down each nice distinction
until the stars we followed are no more
than patterns of the cosmos' DNA.
We found no Eden. We were made this way.

The gifts

We bring the very best things we have made.
We made wealth, lots of it. At first we made it
for our benefit, a mark of fruitfulness,
the limited but real success of the Genesis command;
but then we made it for its own sake, and it grew
like Jack's beanstalk, climbing to the sky,
to a promised kingdom of financial markets,
a world of make-believe where Giant Greed
thunders blindly around looking for lunch.
Sometimes he eats up whole economies
in his hunger for a dividend, yet he dreads
the sound of reality chop-chop-chopping that will pull
the whole thing crashing down about our ears.
We bring our wealth, and our contempt of it.

We made religion, plenty of it. We made it
mainly for our benefit. We shaped it carefully
into Aladdin's lamp, so that when we rub
and say the proper magic words
God rises like a genie from the spout,
our wishes his command. We lie awake
murmuring prayers of *Open Sesame*
for the door of the magic cave to spring
on all the riches of eternity. Sometimes
our fickle genie seems unsatisfied with them and so
we use the lamp more sparingly these days.
We bring religion, and our contempt of it.

We tried to make life, but so far without success.
Determined that like Cinderella we shall go
to the ball of endless youth, the cryogenic fairy waves
her wand of magic promises:

diets, hairdos, workouts, facials,
lifted chins, and now re-engineering—
fresh hips, new lungs, transplanted hearts
and spare part organs grown from embryos
to turn the pumpkin of our body
into a glittering carriage. We don't look bad,
on a good day in a sympathetic light,
but when the clock strikes twelve our time's still up
and our carefully-fashioned show returns
to mice and vegetation. It's a bore.
Prince Charming needn't hold his breath:
we can't yet bring life, and so
we bring death, and our great contempt of it.

The wealth, the incense, the embalming spices,
our pantomime contains the lot.
We hope you like them. They're the best we've got.

The epiphany

A stable is a good place for revelations.
The best discoveries are made in back rooms,
half by accident, by people half-exhausted
and looking for something else.
Just as we felt like giving up,
when the whole thing had become ridiculous
and had gone on much too long, and we were blaming
everybody else for our mistakes,
we came upon an unexpected answer
in the least likely place:
a speechless, thoughtless, helpless child
who just lay there, needing to be loved.
In this defiance of all natural things was born
the enabling power of sacrifice—
a being whose ambition was to seek
his own destruction and then call upon
his followers to do nothing else.
What kind of way was this to rule a world?
He just lay there, needing to be loved.
It would be stopped. Each Herod would conspire
for its destruction, when they cannot tempt it
with possessions nor subdue it with pain
nor lull it to sleep with alcohol or television.
Here was something we could not buy or cure,
digitise, transplant, promote, update, invest in,
analyse or write a business plan for.
He had no army, text-book, voters' mandate
or computer markup language
with which to implement this great design:
he just lay there, needing to be loved.
It was the most implausible demand.
Anything else we could negotiate

but not this secret life secured through death:
grace, born out of deprivation,
grace born of the endurance of the oppressed,
grace born of the hardships of the poor,
grace born of the forgiveness of the intolerable,
grace borne in the dignity of silence, grace born
from incomprehensible submission
to the absolute abuse of power.
In the strength of his weakness
he just lay there, needing to be loved.
Aeons after life exploded into matter
here in this stable was let loose
a far more potent power,
shedding the fabric of his former life
like an old coat, reckless that the truth
would prove for all he knew fatal
to everything to which he had thus far clung.
Our gifts were powerless to help.
There was nothing more to do
but leave the child to his own terrible story,
and return by different routes
to our own countries, strangers to us now,
yet seeing them as if for the first time,
how they just lie there, needing to be loved.

Bernhard Langer approaches Sarajevo

Food convoys part suddenly
revealing Langer
on the 18th tee—

each side of the fairway
in lakes and bunkers
Serbs and Croats lie in ambush—

a crowd of Moslems
holds a strongly fortified position
a good six iron away—

the nations watch,
tortured by handicaps, caddying
for their own agendas—

Joel, three,
assumes the leadership of the western world
and picks up the remote control—

the putt drops, Langer
raises the trophy
in a hundred gunsights.

Truce with the Furies

On the death of R S Thomas

Only time
and our inherited frailty
ended the fight. You were
relentless in pursuit of them, gave
quarter neither to them nor
to the God by whose instruction
or permission they provoked
your Muse to her defiance. They were
your Comforters throughout
that bleak half-century in which you
camped in the machine's detritus,
knowing too well religion's pull
and weakness, kneeling without sentiment upon
the cold flags of your calling to those
whose lives turned on the slow certainties
of harsh work and sly pleasure.

                              Have you now
received your answer, who for all
your pleas and goadings heard
no voice speak its rebuttal from
the whirlwind of your faith's fierce abstention?

Postcards from Florence

1

God doesn't like my hat. The guard
in the Cathedral orders me to take it off,

and so my balding head is cruelly exposed
to His minute examination. Everywhere

sinners in low-cut tops and baggy shorts
flash their Minoltas at the frescoed saints

and leave unjudged. Once the sanctuary was
    approached
one day each year by a single trembling priest,

with certain death the price for anyone
careless enough to touch the covenantal ark

of the same Lord God of Israel
whose dreadful jealousy must now be satisfied

by rage at my straw hat, that cost
twelve thousand lire from a Pisan market stall.

2

Supposedly a pupil somewhere wrote
A vacuum is an empty space occupied by the Pope.

In the church of Santa Croce
we are invited to put coins in slots

and light a timed electric candle on one
of the brazen, gilt madonnas that simper

behind glass panels clutching *bambini* Christs
with the limbs and faces of miniature adults.

Pictures, pictures—none ever seen
by true daylight: Christ in Limbo

amongst the damned, and in judgment in the heavens;
Lucifer falling to a brimstone hell;

and high on the chancel panelling
Eve's painted face contorted by despair.

3

Brunelleschi's Dome was built, like Babel,
to reach a little nearer towards God

than the one in neighbouring Siena.
Donatello's pulpits (*two* of them? in *one* church?) stand

like Martians from Wells' *War of the Worlds*. Pride
and market forces fuelled the Renaissance, and yet

regard the scale of their technology:
their patience hushes the click of the mouse.

Far from the stink of leather in the streets
and the pavement artists chalking out the Masters

—*one photo, one money!*—we browse
Botticelli on CD-ROM and stroll

through a virtual Uffizi, mortals tinkering
with the colours of divinity on our infinite palette of
　　　pixels.

4

Fra Savonarola, Prior of St Marks,
expelled the Medici in 1374, proclaiming

Jesus Christ to be king of Florence, with himself
his political executive, his people drunk

on a fanatic passion. In just four years—
the term of a US President—they had turned, ashamed

at the morning-after evidence of their excess, and
          found
heresies enough to roast him in the same piazza

where so short a time before they burned their pagan
          books,
where we sit now and drink our Pinot Grigiot

and eat *vitello* slightly charred, too late to save
Savonarola, too late to join or reason with the mob

who welcomed back the devil they knew best,
the Medici and their motto: *Semper*, always.

5

The *Deposition* of Fra Angelico
is the painting I love. They pass

Christ's body down between them like a waterfall,
kindness in each expression—saints, apostles, martyrs,

women and Florentine merchants—united
in art as never in life, defying

time to keep them from this act
of corporate obedience. Might it not

as well have happened just like this—the Spirit's
glow in these anachronistic faces, the bell

tolling across the cool cloister of San Marco
as this three-quarter-turned congregation stares out,

pardoning our failures, reborn in this unlikely sacrifice,
brilliant with hope against a Tuscan sky?

No rest for the wicked

If we didn't need sleep just think of all
    each one of us could do—
with eight hours more in twenty-four
    how much we could get through!
Time for working, time for talk
    and lots more time for play,
and all those little jobs you said
    you'd get round to one day!

Pillows may be comforting
    and duvets can be tasteful—
beds have their uses, certainly,
    but sleeping is so *waste*ful!
If you want to get your MBA
    or gain one more diploma
you can't expect to make the grade
    while lying in a coma!

You could be making megabucks,
    instead your broker dozes—
but there'd be no closing market price
    if nothing ever closes!
You could catch up in the rat race
    (though there'd still be more ahead—
I wonder if that's why you never
    see a rat in bed?).

The best of pharmaceutical
    researchers are all hopin'
to find the magic formula
    to keep those eyelids open
before the boys in DNA
    start getting way too clever
and isolate the sleeping gene
    and wake us up for ever!

Are you missing opportunities
    while you're lying there unconscious?
Was Stalin good at breaking eggs?
    Was Pilate's first name Pontius?
We'd boost our productivity
    by staggering proportions—
a third more murders, burglaries
    divorces *and* abortions!

Unending time to monitor
    our share portfolios
it sounds a dream (although of course
    there'd be no more of those!).
But still there's yet another way
    to do it much more neatly:
Let's just cut out the middle man—
    abolish time completely!

Why break our lives up just to fit
   the sun and moon's behaviour?
The timeless web of cyberspace
   can be our virtual saviour!
Weeks are for weaklings, days for the dazed
   and minutes there for taking—
No more seconds, only firsts
   will mark the claims we're staking!

An end at last to jet-lag—
   put that body clock away!
Tomorrow really never comes,
   it's just one long today
No time, no place, no start, no end—
   O wouldn't we be clever
if we didn't need sleep—just think, we could
   live *virtually* for ever...

Galileo and the four moons of Jupiter

He saw the first moon
    Ganymede
bearing the fatal cup
    to Rome's lips.

He saw the second moon
    Callisto
dancing entranced
    around a different god.

With the third moon
    Io
the priest and people sang
    to a universe no longer listening,

and with the fourth moon
    Europa
he knew what had enthralled a continent
    was not worth dying for.

The astronomers

Listen. We hear the background noise
of the beginning of the universe.

It sounds like a worn-out cassette
or the hiss of a snake from a far-off garden.

Look. We see ten billion years
backwards into time.

We are the newest Darwins. Our galaxies
are beautiful flowers of red and blue.

We are virtual explorers. We stay
where we are and bring the universe

to us. We are voyeurs
of the bad habits of constellations: we watch

them grow and marry, then bicker and explode.
Our photographs have given us an idea—

we are remaking the universe
as a theme park. We have made

our calculations. Our prize will be
the film of God, waving to us

across unimaginable space and time.
Somewhere out there we believe is life,

though we are now less certain
of what is left down here.

About time

They have lied to you
about time.

We do not have
time on our hands,
only the scars
left by our grasping at its
unscalable cliffs.

Time is not up
nor on our side.
It moves away from us
into the unknowable future
and the unredeemable past.

Time is not short.
It is as long as memory.

Time is not money.
We cannot save time,
only spend it differently

and time is not running out.
We have too much of it.
Our doctors know that
too much time
kills us all in the end.

Tomorrow always comes.
It's about time
somebody did something
about time.

Strawberry Lodge

*For the re-opening of Carshalton Baptist Church in Strawberry Lodge
after its restoration*

Josias Dewye,
Clothworker and Citizen of London,
lived by blowing people up.
Not directly, of course
(he was a gentleman), but he supplied
Cromwell with England's finest gunpowder
and so became a Guy Fawkes in reverse—
the only man to put an English Parliament
into power with high explosives.

Whether he saw Cromwell
as a just leader, or just a good customer
is not recorded. Dewye weighed out
gunpowder, not principles, and was
too shrewd to bite the hand that fed him.
When the Commonwealth failed, he feared
how Charles the Second might repay
the damage that his products had done
to thousands of his father's loyal subjects—
but Dewye's skills were marketable.
A stickler for production standards
(his victims enjoyed a high quality of death)
he kept his head while all Roundheads
were losing theirs, for Kings need ordnance too.
Dewye was brought to Royalist Carshalton,
revived the powder mills along the Wandle,
took on the Manor House, and made another fortune.
Late in life he built Strawberry Lodge,
but not to live in. Houses are made
for profit or from profit, and this one was both.

He rented it out, made sure his tenants
paid his local taxes, and in old age saw
his daughter married into local gentry,
was honoured Master of his Guild, and died.

What has this to do with us, except to note
that Dewye was a man who took
his opportunities as we do? Arms dealer, landlord,
property developer, skilled at tax avoidance,
he'd be at home today. He was not at heart
religious, and this Lodge was never built
to be a holy house; yet it is one now.
Christ's kingdom doesn't grow
like some rare flower in a peaceful sanctuary
but in the everyday loud, untidy world
of politics and commerce,
where no money is completely clean
and no motive wholly pure. God can take
the best and worst of us and by all means
make something holy, just as this house
has been rebuilt with money earned
in ordinary ways and given for many reasons.
It is a place fit for injured souls and bodies, scarred
in daily civil and uncivil wars. When
we are maimed by loss, or wounded
with indifference or greed, or when
the unstable powder of our pride
blows up in our own faces, we can come here
to learn how life and history can be remade.
After three hundred years the Lodge
stands firm on Dewye's flint foundations,
a parable of Christ's way to build up

his *house of living stones*—stripped down, not bulldozed
but patiently restored to its original design
which centuries of weather and our later
clumsy added-on improvements compromised.
It tells us what we are
is built upon our past, and shows
how something built for profit can be used
for worship, can be transformed into
a property of God's kingdom—and if you think
for you this would take a miracle
then that's his business. It's another joke
in Heaven's upside-down economy
that the gunpowder-maker's final legacy
should be a means of life, not death.
Look round at these solid, beautiful
but guilty walls, redeemed for Christ's service,
and recognise yourself.
You can feel at home here.

Choosing a wife

Choosing a wife is not exactly like choosing
a dog. Look out, naturally,
for bright eyes and well-groomed hair,

but avoid yapping and a wet
nose. Treasure, though,
absolute loyalty and the fetching of slippers

after another day's difficulties; and
choosing a wife is not exactly like choosing
a car. A sporty model, nought to sixty

in a few seconds and responsive
to skilful handling is of course rewarding,
but understand what you may have to pay

in running costs, quite apart from
the constant risk of theft—don't miss
the point, that what matters is

getting from here to there, and the journey
may be long and unpredictable; and then remark
that choosing a wife is not exactly like choosing

a house. Comfort is desirable, and room
for growth and improvement
but do not be fooled by the agent's

carefully-angled photographs;
decide instead how it will look
on a wet November evening

with the kitchen demanding a coat of paint
and the kids avoiding their homework,
and consider the work on your part

needed to make it into
the home you always hope for;
only then will you realise

choosing a wife was much more like
being chosen, and when you weigh up
what's on offer from that perspective

you will be glad that sometimes she lets love
get in the way of her otherwise
unerringly good judgment.

Fancy that

It's hard to be a parent,
keeping up with children's fads—
what a blessing that the telly's
such a help for mums and dads!

How clever that the toys they need
and the drinks and sweets that feed them
are nearly always advertised
just before they need them.

Dark Rider collects the newspaper

On his blue mountain bike,
its white basket tied on with twine
he swoops across the campsite to his prey:

not Darth Vader this morning,
nor Floppy the Seal
nor a nine-year-old boy with a bad dream in the night,

he sings through the walls of the mobile home
and talks relentless nonsense
hoping to throw us off the scent

of his plans for intergalactic supremacy employing
space fighters made from Lego bricks
(powered mainly by carbon).

Taking a fifty franc note from the purse
he pays the scowling Frenchwoman
for two baguettes and yesterday's *Independent*—

she is mercifully unaware of the existence
of the civilization of the Joedasmians
of which he is now the ruthless and absolute ruler.

At Mawgan Porth

Late that first afternoon of holiday
we set off—Emma bright at seven, Joel
determined *nearly four*—to find the path
down to the beach. The bathers were all gone,
and the retreating tide had left a trail
of streams and limpid pools. Emma called out
Follow the river to the sea, and so they went
running and falling in a splash of laughter
to the water's edge. There Joel stood,
Canute-like, to rebuke the indifferent waves,
while I sat down out of the breakers' reach
watching his sister leap in sparkling water,
their shouts ringing across the empty bay.
It may have been no more than the fatigue
of five hours at the wheel, but as I looked
these figures, black against a dazzling sea
cradled between two headlands, heaping sand
into a makeshift fort, brought something
from my mind's eye into focus, and I knew
the phrase's meaning, *I forgot myself*.
The cares, doubts, failures, fights, petty ambitions
that claw like harpies at our blind endeavours
were resting, or had been called off a while,
setting this scene into parentheses
between the unproofed texts of what we were
and what we might become. This was a place
from which innocence had barely taken leave,
like Eden hardly fallen, still uncursed,
as if we did not know there is no cure
for life's long sickness. While I looked it seemed
the sun hung motionless, as once it did
when Joshua fought the Amorites, or so

the story goes, and we were all to be
forever young in health and hope and laughter.
Perhaps God in his dark unravelling
of the virus of the world's misdeeds had paused
to leave one glimpse of grace between
black crags of rock. I had no camera,
but I would not have used it anyway,
for nothing keeps them—sunsets, sandcastles
or children—and I can only follow down
the river of their growing to the sea
of their majority. An hour had passed.
Two distant figures exercised a dog,
quite unaware that on this flat half-mile
of hard, wet sand had been enacted out
a small apocalypse; and walking back, Joel,
plaintive under the weight of plastic spades,
said *It takes a long time, dunt it?* No, Joe,
not nearly long enough; though time will wipe
all but the faintest traces of today
from your encroaching memory as you race
fast forward into a grown-up world, yet when
God, browsing in the ruins of history,
freezes-frame on moments about which
he can say *Here at least I am well pleased*,
then somewhere a man in early middle-age
sits on an almost-empty Cornish beach
watching as two silhouettes play out
their endless childhood in the setting sun,
Joel's wild hair blown like sea-spray in the wind
and Emma dancing on the golden waves.

Harvest

If you would see
these fields full once again
then sow today with quiet words
forgiveness in angry hearts.

Much later it yields
its harvest in our children,
in our ripe and fragile marriages
the amazing crop of grace.

Maureen

She left without fuss
in the greenness of June.

Lads at pub tables
kept mobiles to their ears; girls

downed their glasses of white wine;
kids prepared to leave schools, mums

juggled wants and needs, as they
have always done; middle-aged men

stared into their beers, thinking
they had almost grasped something—

and passed by the church where she was known,
unaware that an old woman had bequeathed

faith like the evening sunlight,
hope like the extravagant green trees

and love like a slow wick in tallow
burning in a thousand hearts.

The Trinity monologue

The Early Fathers of the church, in Asia Minor
(that's Turkey to the likes of you and me)
once decided that nothing would be finer
than to have a get together by the sea.

In AD 325 (or somewhere near)
they found a place with which they were content:
they looked around and said "Well, it's Nicaea—
just the place to have a Council!" —so they went.

They did things to make religion more reliable,
outed heresies and voted bishops in,
even settled on which books make up the Bible—
then sat back and let the great debate begin.

On one side they said that God was undivided;
on the other, Father, Son and Holy Ghost.
For a time it seemed that it would be decided
by the volume of the side that shouted most.

But the Council wouldn't let this fuss defeat it—
a resourceful synod it would prove to be,
for they saw that they could have their cake and eat it
and they came up with the Holy Trinity.

God was One, and he could not be put asunder:
yet His oneness had three persons, they'd evince.
It was settled! They shook hands in peace and
    wonder—
and we've been trying to understand it ever since.

You can think of him as one, and that's no bother;
or you can think of them as three, and that's just fine—
but if you try to mix one thought in with the other
you can never tell where you should draw the line.

Like that picture of the candlestick and faces,
or Escher's stairways that go down yet don't go down,
or like being the same time in different places—
it's just something we can't get our heads around.

For a Hindu, twenty gods are not too many,
while one deity alone's allowed by Jews.
Buddhists calmly smile and say they haven't any
(Jehovah's Witnesses do everything in twos)

but when a Christian tries to do this calculation
it's a method that's old as is the sun:
the answer is to use multiplication—
for 1 times 1 times 1 is always one.

You might think this sleight of hand a bit surprising,
or that theology's completely on the rocks,
but I think our knowledge of our God is rising
when we find we've stumbled on a paradox.

He's a puzzle not for those who are faint-hearted—
he does stuff that can make Einstein look a dunce.
He will finish things before he's even started
and be everywhere—and nowhere—all at once.

It's a riddle that's as elegant as any—
as one person can be body, mind and soul,
as a family is one, and yet is many
so the Godhead is both separate, and whole.

When we try to label, pigeonhole or brand him
and to make God in our image, we've been blind.
Do we really think that we could understand him?
or them? or those? or...oh, look, never mind...

it's a lesson that's been handed down by history—
there's a time to kneel and not keep asking why,
only worship God in all his ancient mystery—
One-in-Three, and out of time...and so am I!

The poem's *cv*

I was born
as a catch in the breath,
the lazy cousin of the parable.

My mission is
to negotiate a settlement
between faith and doubt.

I seem to take seriously
the jargon of the management consultant,
but I am only looking for rhymes.

I feed on imagination.
I am the spending of kinetic energy
like lightning on a sultry night.

I am ambitious.
I am restless for analogy
and sleepless with desire for metaphors.

My principle achievement has been
suspension of belief and disbelief.
My last career will be in science,

weighing the will against the gene, staking out
the infinite distance between co-ordinates
of truth and what now passes for illusion.

Oh, hell

Once upon a time, before Dante's Inferno became a nightclub in Ibiza, on sabbath mornings pulpits across the land blazed with hellfire for forty-five minutes, giving quite a different meaning to the Sunday roast.

Once upon a time, before Demon became an Internet Service Provider, this fear of frying kept us vaguely on the straight and narrow.

Temptation was a dare-devil game. It wasn't entirely clear how close to the flames you were allowed to get and escape with an enviable tan instead of charred and peeling skin.

Absolution was available, but the small print needed good legal advice. The Roman Catholic Church did not fail us. They worked out a full scale of charges and for final settlement negotiated a deal with the authorities—*purgatory*, a sin-bin which God had wisely held back as a negotiating ploy.

But somewhere we stopped feeling comfortable with Hell. Like an embarrassing relative, it was no longer talked about.

What we now know about Hell could be written on the back of a postcard from Southend (and often is). We've heard vaguely of the Seven Deadly Sins: Lust and six others (Dopey, Grumpy, Sneezy, Happy, Bashful and Doc), but The Pit is for Ferraris, and endless torment is just Bosch.

The churches shut their doors, and Hell was homeless.

With Hell gone, Heaven got lazy for lack of competition. Without a Fall there's no-one to pick up, so we are being saved like an account at *Nationwide*. God is our endowment policy, paying the premium for our long-term retirement home.

Meanwhile, no longer welcome in the church, all Hell broke loose and went to Hollywood in search of some attention.

It turned out it had been just a marketing problem: in the right hands Hell became hot property. Scaring people without guilt was child's play (if the child's eyes glowed bright red and its head spun round in circles).

Having conquered mainstream, Hell went ironic as a late night Friday tv quiz game show. *They Think It's All Over (It Certainly Is Now)*.

Hello, good evening and welcome to Better The Devil! *I'm afraid Gabriel has been called away to deal with some Christian Scientists who refuse to believe they're dead. In five minutes when Jesus returns he will be concerned most of all with the sex lives of Catholics. No-one here escapes judgment, except perhaps members of Diocesan Synods who have already endured enough punishment. And now let's see who are this week's sensible sheep and this week's gullible goats . . .*

Wealthy now, Hell poured a fortune out in sponsorship. *Your own Designer hell. Virgin hell is cooler than the rest. Microsoft hell comes with default settings. Mastercard—hell without the waiting.*

To throw the paparazzi off the scent, Hell went on daytime TV to confess how it had betrayed its sex-change lesbian mother's affair with her estranged boyfriend's younger brother's room-mate's Siamese twin who had been secretly engaged all the time to her plastic surgeon's rent-boy's dad.

Hell sneaked out in the confusion to check in for detox with a secret stash of heroin, and a contract with *Hello* magazine for the photographs.

Hell tried sport, but didn't like the rules.

Hell found war much more promising. It set off global arguments like a juggler spinning plates.

Behind the headlines things were going nicely. Style's hell had children sewing training shoes for twelve hours every day. Fashion's hell was sick with anorexic teenage girls. Narcotic hell grew like a tumour. African hell spread like a virus. American hell was paralysed by endless choice. British hell remained generally undecided about the merits of a single European currency.

Hell had risen without trace. The best was yet to come. It had found at last a place to call its own.

It has spent a lot of money on its website. It has great graphics. It has a famous Nickname.

Reality just took a standing count. Hell has found the killer application. It waits for us to log on.

Normandy

Each day at Bayeux the invasion fleet—
magnificent in woven green and gold—

sails to its bloody destiny to free
England from a coming age of darkness;

and hourly at Arromanches the invasion fleet—
in IMAX vision and surrounding sound—

steams to its bloody destiny to free
England from a coming age of darkness

and plough back Norman blood into this landscape—
as grey as newsreel, flat as tapestry—

and always here at Douvres-la-Délivrande
British and German souls lie quietly,

all conquest done, ambition satisfied,
mingled in European earth forever.

Possibly a Celtic invocation

The clay breaks,
light shines through.

The heart breaks,
Love shines through.

31.12.99

In the afternoon we pushed through the funfair on the
    Mall,
went twice on one of the less gravitationally-challenging
    rides,

saw a tv personality on a big screen in the sunset in
    Trafalgar Square
and rode back on the Piccadilly Line for the early
    evening service at St Mary's,

where a few dozen sat quietly to hear the old familiar
    promises
and shrug off the weight of resolutions unmade or
    unkept—

a conspiracy of silence with the shared alibi of being
    human—
travelling back later for the fireworks with thousands
    making determined pilgrimage

and looking for meaning in the rollover of figures,
gazing upwards into the sky

not at an apocalypse bursting like bombs above
    Baghdad or Kosovo
but a harmless display, famous for fifteen minutes,
    visible from outer space

to catch the eye of any passing god accepting
    worshippers at this point in time,
while down here each watches from his or her vantage
    point—

myidentity@anywhere.com in y2k version 1.0—
as the digital nightmare of the 21st century opens up
    like a lapdancer:

on Millennium Eve a planetful of celebrants exiled
    from one another
search for something which is not found in the image
    of the couple at Green Park,

the woman pleading and brushing away tears,
the man's face immobile, set against the unattainable
    truth of a century's high water mark,

the notion *All you need is love*—
stupid, naïve in execution if not in concept,

a cry of hope vanishing in bangs and flashes:
as we escape, the virus of the old century is smuggled
    in in the bloodstream of the new.

Gironde

A dry track runs through pines along the shore
where the roots hold the sand together.

The lighthouse wipes the sky and washes
the moon's cracked face. Tonight its beams

pick out no horsemen. Life is change,
and change is just a line of little deaths

whispering like the wind high in these trees
Life cannot be lived except

in dying. In a season such as this
the soul may shrink and dry like leather

becoming a hard, small ball,
something to be thrown and hit

beyond who-knows-what boundary
if not caught in love's firm glove.

Skin

That Christmas, God treated himself to a new coat. Till then he'd not really been dressed for visiting. He had nothing dull enough to wear.

Quite early he had come to realise that his appearance wasn't likely to put people at their ease. Even the very first ones were nervous. When he went for an afternoon stroll around the garden, they would run and hide.

And those times when he showed someone around, he had to admit their reactions were hardly reassuring. He saw it must be a little difficult to be wholly relaxed in the presence of a host with dazzling white hair, emerald eyes and a tongue like a sword, seated on a blazing throne guarded by four six-winged living creatures and two dozen elders chanting incessantly. Polite, yes, but probably not relaxed. Likely to slop tea onto the chocolate digestives.

So he took to meeting just a trusted few, in places carefully arranged—a mountain or a desert, away from crowds. He made them build a tent, for conferences, with heavily restricted access. When he spoke, he found the quiet voices worked best.

Eventually it became easier just to send a messenger. Of course people were still startled when a shining creature several metres high materialised in their living rooms like something from the Starship Enterprise, but they did their job. And angels don't have feelings you can hurt.

He learned that people were more comfortable with their own kind. Pleased when you showed an interest, of course, but when the boss from the top floor drops by the conversation's always stilted, and both sides are relieved when he's gone.

So when the time came for the business that had to be done, he went incognito. Dressing down for the occasion, he chose skin. Not suede or leather, just skin. Close-fitting, durable, anonymous, adaptable. No special style or colour.

Skin was his lifetime companion. He nursed the scabs of childhood games on his knees and elbows. He felt the muscles growing inside it, the ligaments stretch when he extended himself. He fingered the callouses made by a workman's tools on his palms.

He came to know skin from the inside. He knew the pleasant shock of cold water splashed across his face in the midday heat. He knew the touch of cool parchment unrolling beneath his fingertips, the dryness in his mouth as he prepared to read what was written there about him.

He noticed skin harden under feet that walk long distances. After sleepless nights he felt it hang in folds beneath his eyes. When he was most tired it felt almost detached from him, a loose sack keeping him warm.

Once, when he thought he had won their confidence enough, he gave three of them a glimpse of his real appearance. They were terrified, and he never risked it again.

He saw skin made repulsive by disease, and healed it. He saw Lazarus walking, and felt a ripple of gooseflesh on his spine.

He knew the feel of an animal's rough back beneath his thighs, and breezes from waving branches. When anger sluiced blood to the surface of the skin he felt his face flush red.

He watched how liquids trickled over it. He could tell the different tensions of tears and ointment as they ran down his cheeks and beard.

He washed skin carefully, his own and others'. He saw how it protected them, the tiny beads of water dripping from their feet into his bowl. He knelt on dew-drenched grass and felt his cloak cling round his legs. His burning forehead prickled with cold drops of fear.

He felt how, when whipped repeatedly, skin disintegrates and the soft flesh underneath is ploughed up like a bright red field. He knew then how necessary it had been. Skin had dulled the pain of being a man, and kept the parts together long enough. Now it was time to shed it. It was torn in strips from his back, gouged out of the palms of his hands, and pierced so that fluids would spill out more easily. At the end he saw it was no more than a ripped bag bursting with offal, cut down and wrapped like meat to put into cold storage.

It was finished. What would happen next, even he did not exactly know, but he had watched creatures discard their coats in preparation for something. He was ready for a new and different skin.

The driving seat

Have you ever ridden on the back seat, Dad?

Yes, I've ridden on the back seat—

As a child
I rode on the back seat
going on holiday, with my parents up in front.
As in a dream I heard their voices far away,
talking about me.

As a teenager
I rode on the back seat,
in the comforting dark
of a carful of bodies crushed together,
restless with new feelings.

At my father's funeral
I rode on the back seat,
too old for childish tears, too young
to wear with ease the hour's solemnity.

Nowadays
in cars to the airport in the early morning
I ride on the back seat,
with my suitcase, passport, currency,
my schedule printed neatly by my assistant,

but today
I'm in the driving seat.

One day I expect
I shall ride again on the back seat.
Maybe you'll be at the wheel.
I'll hear your voices far away,
talking about me.

But for today
I'm in the driving seat.

Ride on

They're waving at you.
Ride on.

Some wave to flag you down
like witnesses at a motorway pile-up.
They want to you to fix the injured and dying.
You can cure them.
You can bring the dead back to life.

Ride on.

Some are waving Hello.
They want you to come to their party.
They want to show you off to their friends.
They know some very open-minded Pharisees.
They are sure they will be reasonable about it
once you explain.

Ride on.

Some wave the team colours.
They want you to stuff the opposition,
they think its time that our guys won.

Ride on.

Some wave business cards.
They want you to endorse their products.
You are hot property for chat shows.
Your position statements will be prepared for you.
You will be dressed by Armani and Calvin Klein
for your limitless media opportunities.

Ride on.

Some wave to warn you.
They want you to take care.
They'd like to re-direct your route
away from likely trouble spots.
They have your best interests at heart.

Ride on.

Some wave in desperation as if
you are their only hope.

Ride on.

Some wave their fists.
You were the wrong answer to their prayers
and their disappointments have blossomed into anger.
You could have sorted out the whole bloody mess
and here you are out donkey-riding.

Ride on.

Ride on until
the temple looms in front of you.
Dismount.
Walk the last few steps
towards the tables
where religion is prepared.
Push them all over.
Leave no room for doubt.

Walk into
the dark garden,
the false kiss,
the clever trap,
the rigged trial,
the beating,
the goading.
Stop for nothing
and at nothing
and when you have nothing left to give
give all that you have.

Judas calls Room Service

On channel 42
the preachers—
black and white,
men and women—

expound/amplify/
elucidate/spell out
every meaning
under the sun,

sluicegates of words
poured out amidst
his inexplicable miracles
of grace.

My faith
is in Room Service,
running through my order
like a thesaurus—

I take salvation over easy
on white bread,
and raid the minibar for wine.
I thirst.

Communiqué

In the end we have to state
that no agreement was reached.
His stubborn opposition to compromise
was never breached.

Talks went on through the night
to meet Friday's deadline.
Even the governor was woken early
to sign.

But no peace formula was found
at the eleventh hour.
Between the princes of earth and of heaven
there will be no sharing of power.

Every effort was made
to break down his reticence
but he would not join in any talks
and maintained his silence.

The release of prisoners
was the final opportunity.
It is reported that he did not take advantage
of the governor's offer of clemency.

There is no bilateral statement
for the six o'clock news.
The communiqué that was displayed
said simply, *He is the King of the Jews*.

On reflection it is clear
his agenda had been set from the start.
He planned a suicide mission
against the strongholds of the heart.

He did not negotiate with sin
when matters reached their head.
He would not de-commission his arms
but spread them wide instead.

The cure

Wondering, she watched as arm in arm they drew
towards the car, walking so silently.

Her nerves stretched taut as an elastic band.
The February day grew monochrome.

What's next? she said, braced for the brutal cure
of radio- or chemo-therapy;

but her friend smiled her brave, familiar smile:
Heaven's next was all she said. And they drove home.

Fixed

Between time and eternity
nothing was fixed.
One gaped at the other
across the unbridgeable void.

Stories of patriarchs
pinned them lightly together.
A loose frame of parables,
scraps of psalms,
prophecies,
tongues.

Poets tried words.
Scientists, numbers.
Musicians, delicate vibrations.
Painters, the placing of colours,

but nothing was fixed
until a workman took
a hammer and a wrist
and with one whack nailed down
eternity screaming into time.

Only wood

Which door is it behind?
Where did they hide the good?
Try them, you'll find
they're only wood.

A choice of empty promises,
a way of passing time.
Fashion, illusion,
a passionless crime.

If one of them should speak
and say *I am the door*
then I might listen, I might wonder
what the rigmarole was for.

But what kind of door would speak?
Not one that's only wood
but one hinged on eternity
and framed in flesh and blood.

On what scene would it open?
What agony would face
this splintered human door
that must be hung and hammered into place?

I've heard that voice,
I know that broken door, and I'm afraid
not only of the broken wood
but of the shape in which it's made.

From where she lies

From where she lies the view is lovely.
You can see the valley from here.
Beside her, carefully-chosen cards
don't say *Get Well Soon*.

We come and go, not knowing
which goodbye will be goodbye.
For a few days she seems stateless.
The angels are checking her passport.

They needn't fret. She has
the necessary visa. Even here
she wears the bittersweet, regretful grace
of an ambassador returning home.

The pain is nothing, she says,
and now for her the world is nothing,
and from where she lies the view is lovely.
You can see heaven from here.

Five candles

Eleven o'clock. Twenty chairs. A book
lies open at some fitting passages
and, in a covered case, a register.
The awkward, gentle, sympathetic words
that tiptoe round the possibility
of perfect, quite untenable despair. Our eyes
are drawn towards a simple stem from which
five candles rise in step into the centre.
First Laura Beth, then John, then dad and mum
hold matches out until five flames rise steadily
for Luke, the object of this holy sadness
who never breathed with us our troubled air:
and so a family is defined.
                          Meanwhile outside
the lorries rumble past—the peaceful dead can't stop
the noisy work of tending to the living.
The half-hour service done, a dozen guests
walk out into the garish August sun
to private cares and wounded lives. Death
is a great healer and the acid test of love.
Not even nights of utter desolation
can keep us from the savage care of Christ,
but prove the miracle that faith is born
as a child of grief, and the foul-tasting cup
of suffering's the medicine of heaven. To those
in the material world who say that life
is just the sum of our activity,
and in their cruellest kindnesses insist
an unborn child is no more than a thing;
and do not know how love can turn
a hospital's prefabricated room
to sacred ground, or how a flame may burn

and never be consumed—to them these five
blue candles will forever give the lie.

Postmodern

Science with the brakes gone
careers through our mental undergrowth

leaving a trail of trampled world-views.
Each new release of the mind's operating system

is incompatible with the last. Language
follows science at the unsafe distance

of too many generations—words,
set spinning by Copernicus,

pulled down to earth by Newton,
made relative by Einstein, are uncertain now

as quantum mechanics, exploded by Hubble into
an infinite number of possible forms, each syllable

moving away from its companion
at breakneck speed. Our grasp

of meaning loosens, the normal tools of language
are cast aside, and cannot hold

the delicately fractured syllogisms or predict
the consequences of this status quo

where cause becomes effect, the universe
an echo of David Hume's reluctant laughter. Darwin,

Marx, Freud and Wittgenstein, this church of latter-day
saints who thought they had destroyed it

find they have only ripped off more of the mask
of time's accretions, helping us to see

that face in all its unfamiliarity—
the face of God in a set

of perfect numbers—one and zero,
all or nothing, *formless and empty, darkness*

on the surface of the deep, the Spirit hovering
over the waters—falling in a rain of superstrings

under whose downpour our pedestrian words
huddle against drowning like dumb creatures

safe in their ark of paradox. Close to the end
or the beginning we are not surprised to find

myth and mathematics the only languages
we are able to comprehend, the blank equations

sprawling across infinite whiteboards to where
the text of Genesis awaits its final discovery.

Postscript

It's so confusing
these days now
things move so fast and
everything's been
reinvented,
it's hard to find
time to understand
all the new
words while keeping
up with life's daily
demands, so I made
a Post-it list
of things I must
sort out post-
haste: post-
modern, post-
evangelical, post
that cheque to
British Telecom
before they cu

Notes for performance

Some of the pieces in this book were written specifically for performance and some may be performed effectively using two or more voices, or with other contextual or visual aids. I have provided some notes below on a number of pieces which can benefit from a degree of direction or multiple voices, but would-be readers or performers are free to use their imagination to use the material in other ways. Many are most effective when learned and spoken or acted without having to be read. It is sometimes appropriate to substitute local references (for example, a local traffic black-spot for the Wandsworth one-way system) but otherwise please resist the temptation to try to "improve" on the poems.

Copies of some of some of these pieces marked up as scripts for two or more voices are available free by email (or send sae) from Wordsout.

Adore your door can be done effectively in the style of a television appeal, using up to three speakers sitting behind a desk.

Communiqué should be read (not spoken) in the matter-of-fact, knowing manner of an official press spokesperson.

Light of the world was written for two characters, one the leader and the second his somewhat facetious assistant. They are equipped with pens/pencils and clipboards to which the script for the Nativity is (apparently) attached, and as they read through and discuss this they make notes on their copies of the script.

The **Magi** sequence was originally written for and read by two voices, one male and one female, as four separate readings providing a narrative framework for a carol service. The poems can be broken up into parts shared more or less randomly by the voices, who represent the Magi. Any number of readers could be used (I think it would be very effective with half a dozen) but *not* three.

Ride on works with two voices, one speaking only the phrase "Ride on" and then the final section of the poem

Song at the start of a century is for two or more voices. The simplest arrangement is for the second voice to speak the sections in italics. Although serious in subject, this poem should be fast-moving and entertaining.

The last straw is a series of eight brief introductions to Christmas Bible readings, which can be used in a carol service format as prologues to the readings themselves, in place of the traditional sentence of explanation. The same person should read all the poems and act as a narrator, while the Bible readings may be read by different people. The fact that there are eight poems, while the traditional carol service has nine lessons, should act as a challenge to creativity! The poems can of course be used on their own.

The Trinity Monologue is written in the style of the music hall monologues (such as *Albert and the Lion*) made famous by Stanley Holloway and should be read in this manner if at all possible.

I don't believe any of the pieces in this book are inherently unperformable, but I would be very interested to see a live interpretation of **Signs** or **An exponent of the Prosperity Gospel replies to the Beatitudes!**

Index of Themes

This listing has been compiled to help those looking for material to read or perform in the context of services or events, so pieces are listed against themes or seasons which may be most useful. It is not intended as a comprehensive subject index: it only includes pieces which were either written for performance or which work effectively when spoken.

GR